# Standards-Based
# MATH
## Graphic Organizers, Rubrics, and Writing Prompts for Middle Grade Students

By Imogene Forte
and Sandra Schurr

Incentive Publications, Inc.
Nashville, Tennessee

*Graphics by Joe Shibley*
*Cover by Marta Drayton*
*Edited by Jean K. Signor*

ISBN 0-86530-491-2

1   2   3   4   5   6   7   8   9   10        07    06    05    04

PRINTED IN THE UNITED STATES OF AMERICA
www.incentivepublications.com

# Table of Contents

# PREFACE

Recent research studies have confirmed a belief that intuitive teachers have long held germane to classroom success: when students are meaningfully involved in active learning tasks and in the planning and evaluation of their work, they are more enthusiastic about instructional activities, they learn and retain more, and their overall rate of achievement is greater. With the emphasis placed on measurable achievement as an overriding goal driving school system mandates, curriculum, classroom organization and management, and even instructional practices and procedures, teachers are faced with great challenges. While striving to fulfill societal demands, at the same time they must be creating and using new instructional strategies, procedures, and teaching methods to meet the diverse needs of students with widely varying interests and abilities. With the complexity of daily life in the rapidly changing world in which we live, the global economy, and the growing avalanche of information, middle grades math teachers are turning to student-centered instruction, active learning strategies, and authentic instruction to capture and hold students' interests and attention, and consequently to result in increased achievement levels.

## Graphic Organizers

As the body of material to be covered in a given time frame grows more massive and multifaceted, and content demands on students and teachers multiply, graphic organizers are becoming an important component of middle grades math programs.

In the information-saturated classroom of today, sorting and making meaningful use of specific facts and concepts is becoming an increasingly important skill. Knowing where to go to find information and how to organize it once it is located is the key to processing and making meaningful use of the information gathered. Graphic organizers can be used to: provide visual organization; develop scope and sequence; furnish a plan of action or to aid in assessment; clarify points of interest; and document a process or a series of events.

Their construction and use encourages visual discrimination and organization, use of critical thinking skills, and meta-cognitive reflection. They can be particularly useful in helping middle grade students grasp concepts and skills related to the thirteen standards established by the National Council of Teachers of Mathematics.

In other instances, a graphic organizer may be developed as a reporting or review exercise or sometimes as a means of self-assessment when properly used after knowledge has been acquired. Graphic organizers become a valuable and effective instructional and assessment tool. The degree of their effectiveness for both students and teachers is determined by clarification of purpose, careful planning, visual organization, and attention to detail.

## Rubrics

Authentic assessment, as opposed to more traditional forms of assessment, gives both student and teacher a more realistic picture of gains made, facts, and information processed for retention. Emphasis is placed more on the processing of concepts and information than on the recall of facts. Collecting evidence from authentic assessment exercises, taking place in realistic settings over a period of time, provides students and teachers with the most effective documentation of both skills and content mastery. Traditional measurements of student achievement such as written tests and quizzes, objective end-of-chapter tests, and standardized tests play a major role in the assessment picture as well.

The use of standards-based rubrics in middle grade math classes has proven to be an extremely useful means of authentic assessment for helping students maintain interest and evaluate their own progress.

Rubrics are checklists that contain sets of criteria for measuring the elements of a product, performance, or portfolio. They can be designed as a qualitative measure (holistic rubric) to gauge overall performance of a prompt, or they can be designed as a quantitative measure (analytic rubric) to award points for each of several elements in response to a prompt.

Additional benefits from rubrics are that they: require collaboration among students and teachers; are flexible and allow for individual creativity; make room for individual strengths and weaknesses; minimize competition; are meaningful to parents; allow for flexible time frames; provide multifaceted scoring systems with a variety of formats; can be sources for lively peer discussions and interaction; can include meta-cognitive reflection provisions which encourage self-awareness and critical thinking; and can help teachers determine final grades that are understood by and hold meaning for students.

## Writing Prompts

Over the past several years, the significance of journals and writing prompts is well-documented by student and teacher observations. When students write about experiences, knowledge, hopes, fears, memories, and dreams, they broaden and clarify skills and concepts while acquiring new insights into themselves and the big world of which they are a part.

While random journal entries hold their own place of importance in the math classroom, writing prompts designed to elicit specific responses play a vital role in the instructional program.

Journal entries may be presented in many different formats, and may be shared and assessed in a variety of ways. The flexibility of their use and the possibilities they provide for integrating instruction cause them to be viewed as an important component of the personalized math program. They may take the form of a file card project, a multimedia presentation, a special notebook, or a diary. They may be private, to be discussed with the teacher only, shared with a small group of peers, or with the total class. Word prompts can be used in parent-student-teacher conferences, or as take-home projects to be shared with parents, saved, or used as a portfolio entry to give an account of a unit of study, field trip, or independent project.

Writing prompts provide the opportunity for students to: create a dialogue with teachers in a meaningful sense; write about self-selected topics of high interest; process and internalize material being learned; communicate with peers; express private opinions, thoughts, and insights without judgment or censorship; write personal reactions or responses to textbook, research assignments, group discussion, and experiences; make record of what and how they are learning and what it means to them; develop a source book of ideas and thoughts related to a specific topic; question material being studied and record answers as they are uncovered; assess their academic or social progress; and engage in meta-cognitive reflection on new skills and concepts being acquired. They are also recording plans for further exploration.

These standards-based graphic organizers, writing prompts, and rubrics have been designed to provide busy teachers with a bank of resources from which to draw as the need arises. The thirteen standards developed by the National Council of Teachers of Mathematics have been incorporated throughout all activities. For ease in planning, the matrix on pages 118–121 provides a complete correlation of activities to these standards.

# Graphic Organizers

# GUIDELINES
## FOR USING GRAPHIC ORGANIZERS

1. Graphic organizers have many purposes; they can be used for curriculum planning, helping students process information, and pre- or post-assessment tasks. Determine which types of graphic organizers are best for each purpose.

2. Graphic organizers are a performance-based model of assessment and make excellent artifacts for inclusion in a portfolio. Decide which concepts in your discipline are best represented by the use of these organizers.

3. Use graphic organizers to help students focus on important concepts while omitting extraneous details.

4. Use graphic organizers as visual pictures to help the student remember key ideas.

5. Use graphic organizers to connect visual language with verbal language in active learning settings.

6. Use graphic organizers to enhance recall of important information.

7. Use graphic organizers to provide student motivation and relieve student boredom.

8. Use graphic organizers to show and explain relationships between and among varied content areas.

9. Use graphic organizers to make traditional lesson plans more interactive and more appealing to the visual learner.

10. Use graphic organizers to break down complex ideas through concise and structured visuals.

11. Use graphic organizers to help students note patterns and clarify ideas.

12. Use graphic organizers to help students better understand the concept of part to whole.

13. Emphasize the use of graphic organizers to stimulate creative thinking.

14. Make sure there is a match between the type of organizer and the content being taught.

15. Make sure that using a graphic organizer is the best use of time when teaching a concept.

16. Use a wide variety of graphic organizers and use them collaboratively whenever possible.

*Standards-Based MATH Graphic Organizers, Rubrics, and Writing Prompts for Middle Grade Students*

# The ABC's of an Important Math Topic/Standard

**DIRECTIONS:** Choose a key math topic or standard that you are studying and record an important fact, example, definition, comment, or piece of information that you want to remember about it.

Use the ABC outline to help organize your thoughts.

See page 24 for reproducible copy.

### The ABC's of An Important Math Topic/Standard

A _____
B _____
C _____
D _____
E _____
F _____
G _____
H _____
I _____
J _____
K _____
L _____
M _____
N _____
O _____
P _____
Q _____
R _____
S _____
T _____
U _____
V _____
W _____
X _____
Y _____
Z _____

# Biography of a Mathematician Organizer

**DIRECTIONS:** The biography organizer is useful for organizing major facts of a specific life story. Students may use it as a writing aid for sorting out information and events related to the subject's life in preparation for writing the most interesting biography possible. This is especially true when the study allows for use of a variety of resource materials that need to be clarified and coordinated to provide details, as well as eliminate overlap or redundancy of facts and information.

See page 25 for reproducible copy.

A Biography of: _____

| | |
|---|---|
| Place/Date of Birth | |
| Family History | |
| Early Life | |
| Education | |
| Major Actions | |
| Major Events | |
| Major Influences | |
| Major Contributors | |
| Major Friends | |
| Major Problems | |
| Famous Quotes or Words | |

# Brainstorming Web

This web can be used as an effective planning tool for cooperative learning groups, peer tutoring, or class discussion. It may be especially valuable for recording spontaneous responses in problem solving settings and as a follow-up organizational framework for sorting out and making meaningful use of the recorded information. It may also be used as a planning outline for an individual student report or research project. In this instance, it might be included in the student portfolio as part of the planning process and as a component of the assessment criteria.

See page 26 for reproducible copy.

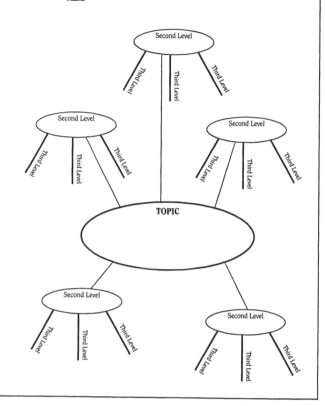

# Brochure Building

Using a brochure format to outline one's thoughts about mathematics is a good way to explore, convey, and clarify mathematical concepts and ideas. Duplicate the graphic organizer below, fold the sections on the dotted lines, and complete each of the six sections (three per side) following these guidelines for recording and discussing your thoughts. Label each section 1 through 6.

Section 1: Write your name, date, and the math-related topic for this brochure.

Section 2: Write down a series of important facts or key things to remember about this topic.

Section 3: Write down some specific and concrete examples of this topic in action to show how it works.

Section 4: Write out some questions you might ask of others to test what they know about this topic.

Section 5: Write down the correct answers to these questions that you would accept as valid.

Section 6: Construct a drawing or model of something related to this topic.

See page 27 for reproducible copy.

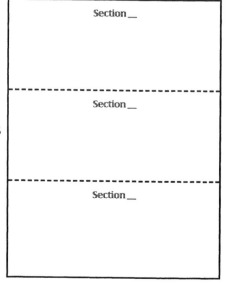

# Calendar Organizer

The simple calendar organizer is a valuable organizational tool for use on all content areas, but especially for math. First, a study of the calendar and its history and use through the ages provides insights into the value of numbers and the numerical system to science, history, and world cultures as defined by common understandings. The blank calendar may be used to create a portfolio artifact, to serve as the basis of an outline or a timeline for a project or course of study as a record-keeping device for homework or classroom assignments, as a peer tutoring or cooperative learning aid, or as an instructional tool.

A word-a-day calendar (using words from the lists on pages 122–123), a symbol-a-day calendar (using symbols from page 125), a problem-a-day calendar, or a famous mathematician-of-the-day calendar might be constructed to extend classroom use of math skills and concepts as well as to provide icebreakers and sparkers for additional incentive and enthusiasm. The two calendars, A Calendar of Writing Sparkers (page 132) and the Take Ten Calendar (page 133) will serve as models for developing new ones in keeping with interests unique to each classroom.

See page 28 for reproducible copy.

# Checklist of Questions To Answer When Studying From Math Textbook

DIRECTIONS: Gathering and interpreting information from chapters in a textbook (or any other math resource of information) requires a process that is both reliable and manageable.

These questions should help you grasp the most important points. Check off each question as you are able to answer it while reviewing the written material.

See page 29 for reproducible copy.

|  |
| --- |
| What is my purpose for reading this material? Notes: |
| What do I already know about this topic? Notes: |
| What are the guiding questions I need to be able to answer on this topic? Notes: |
| What information is most important here? Notes: |
| What questions does this information raise for me? Notes: |
| How can I organize this information so I can remember it more easily? Notes: |
| How can I visualize or picture this information? Notes: |
| What do I want to discuss with my teacher or my class about this information? Notes: |

# Data Graph

The Data Graph is a tool for collecting and organizing numerical information so that it can be used to draw conclusions and report findings. This organizer can be used to compile data on a variety of topics and then to show or display the information using the format of a bar graph, circle graph, line graph, or picture graph.

See page 30 for reproducible copy.

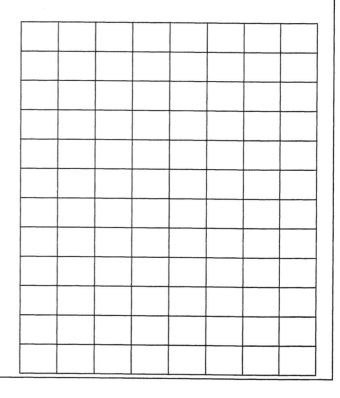

# Decision Chart

The Decision Chart is helpful when you have to make a decision or solve a problem and you do not know quite where to begin. In the DECISION rectangle at the top of the page, write a brief statement that describes the nature of the decision you must make or the problem to be solved. Then, in the ALTERNATIVE IDEAS column, list a number of alternative ideas that could resolve your dilemma.

Then decide on a set of criteria to be used in judging the worth of each alternative idea and list these in the slanted boxes labeled CRITERIA. Rate each individual criterion according to the scoring scale as shown. Finally, compile the total score for each alternative idea. The best decision is probably the idea that has the highest point value!

See page 31 for reproducible copy.

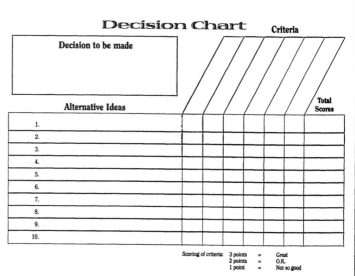

# Fact and Information Organizer

Use the Fact and Information Organizer to organize information and structure your ideas or to support a hypothesis. The major topic is written in the oval at the top of the tree, subheadings in other ovals, and facts and information on diagonals extending from the subheadings. This graphic organizer is especially useful for organizing and making meaningful use of a vast and unwieldy amount of information on a given subject as it can help to cut out less important facts and information and highlight the important.

See page 32 for reproducible copy.

# Filmstrip Organizer

Use the various sections of the filmstrip organizer below to draw and describe how mathematical concepts relate to other subject areas you study in school or how they relate to their everyday lives. Draw a different picture or diagram in each frame and then write a simple sentence under each frame that states the real world application or connection. This organizer may be duplicated several times to add extra frames as needed for the reporting of your information.

See page 33 for reproducible copy.

# Flowchart

Flowcharts are used to organize sequences of events, actions, or decisions. A standards set of symbols is used when designing flowcharts so that all can understand them. The arrangement of the symbols will vary according to the type of sequence depicted. A Flowchart can be especially valuable for finding answers to questions or solving problems. The question to be answered or the problem to be solved is written in the diamond with yes/no responses recorded in circles, action steps in rectangles, explanations in broken-line rectangles, and answers in trapezoids. The flowchart is a valuable aid for choosing operations for solving a word problem.

See page 34 for reproducible copy.

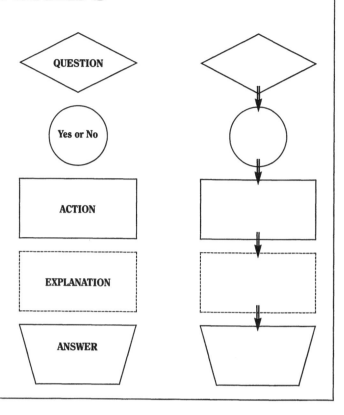

# Graph Matrix

The graph matrix has many uses for the math student. It provides a starter matrix to use when constructing a bar graph or a line graph. One set of descriptors is placed on the vertical axis and another set of descriptors on the horizontal axis to show the relationship between the two categories.

See page 35 for reproducible copy.

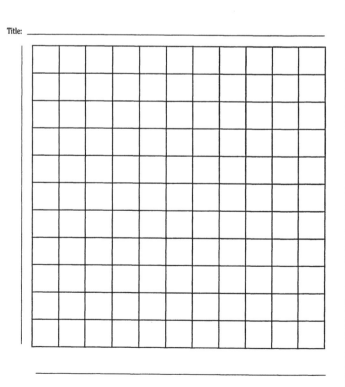

# Math Portfolio or Project Plan

When properly used, the Math Portfolio or Project Plan can serve to clarify and make record of agreed upon learning goals, dates, materials needed, plan of action and method of assessment for the project. In addition to providing a guide for the student, it provides a common understanding and consistent reminders of both student and teacher expectancies.

See page 36 for reproducible copy.

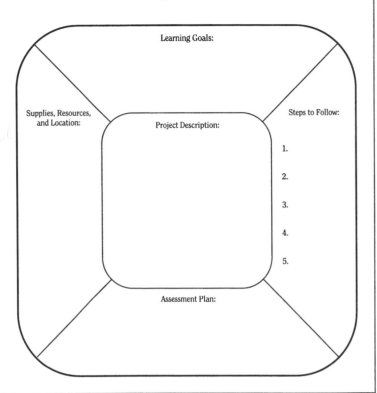

# Math Project Planning Tool

Use the Math Project Planning Tool for planning and completing a project that has a major goal and subgoals to be accomplished through the completion of a variety of sequential tasks. The major goal is written in the large box and the subgoals in the medium-sized boxes. The sequence of tasks is then organized in the smaller boxes to be carried out. It is important that each set of tasks be grouped with the appropriate subgoal in the diagram.

See page 37 for reproducible copy.

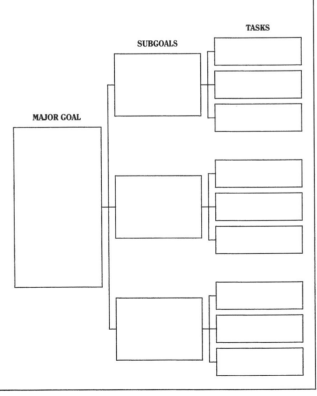

# Math Research Study Plan

This planning form may be used to map out a game plan for completing an independent study of a specific topic. Since this planning form is flexible in nature to allow for individual creativity, it is important that specific details and plans for completing the study be recorded.

See page 38 for reproducible copy.

**PERSONAL PROJECT PLAN**

| Title and Description of Study | Beginning Date | Format for Study |
|---|---|---|
| | —— | |
| | Completion Date | |
| | —— | |

Resources Needed and Location

Challenges to be expected and/or questions to answer

Method of Evaluation

# Math Vocabulary Learning Ladder

The Math Vocabulary Learning Ladder is a good tool to keep in a notebook and use on a regular basis during class instruction, as well as for homework and independent assignments. Its use is self-explanatory and provides a convenient record of student progress in making efficient use of new words and terms. A completed learning ladder makes a valuable artifact for a math portfolio or appendix item for an independent project.

See page 39 for reproducible copy.

Word or Term: _____
Textbook Sentence: _____
Page: _____ Definition: _____
_____
**5**
Word or Term: _____
Textbook Sentence: _____
Page: _____ Definition: _____
_____
**4**
Word or Term: _____
Textbook Sentence: _____
Page: _____ Definition: _____
_____
**3**
Word or Term: _____
Textbook Sentence: _____
Page: _____ Definition: _____
_____
**2**
Word or Term: _____
Textbook Sentence: _____
Page: _____ Definition: _____
_____
**1**

# Mind Map

A Mind Map is a graphic illustration of major ideas around a central topic or theme. Mind maps are useful tools in helping us draw a global picture of a concept for ourselves. The steps for constructing a mind map:

1. In the middle of the page, write out the major topic, idea, or concept to be studied. Put a colored circle around the topic.

2. Identify subtopics related to the main idea in the circle. Write down a key word or brief phrase describing each subtopic. Circle each subtopic with a colored pencil and draw a spoke out from the main idea. Put related ideas in circles of the same color. Keep the number of key words/phrases to a minimum.

See page 40 for reproducible copy.

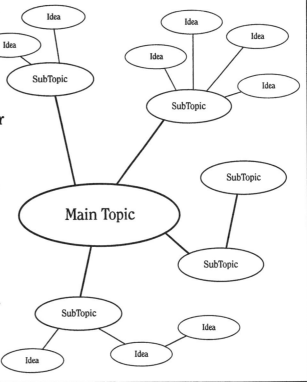

# Prediction Web

The Prediction Web is a valuable tool for organizing facts and information to arrive at or support a prediction. Write the major topic or problem under discussion as a question in the square box at the bottom of the tree. Brainstorm possible predictions or probable outcomes in response to the question and record these in the prediction boxes. On the proof lines, record facts that either support or negate the predictions.

See page 41 for reproducible copy.

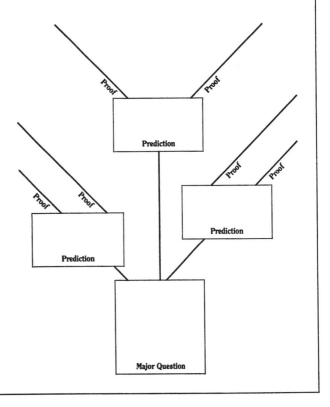

*Standards-Based MATH Graphic Organizers, Rubrics, and Writing Prompts for Middle Grade Students*

# Problem-Solution Boxes

Math word problems are recorded in a box located in the PROBLEM column.

In the HOW SOLVED column, write the operation(s) required to solve the problem along with your own computation.

This is an organizer to be kept in the math notebook for use as a valuable study guide, as well as surviving as a record of work done. It may also serve as an artifact for a math portfolio.

See page 42 for reproducible copy.

| PROBLEM | HOW SOLVED |
| --- | --- |
|  |  |
|  |  |
|  |  |
|  |  |

# Problem Star Organizer

The Problem Star Organizer encourages students to consider various points or solutions to a specific problem under study. The problem is written in the center of the star. The key points to consider, steps to follow to solve the problem, or potential solutions to the problem are written on the five points of the star.

See page 43 for reproducible copy.

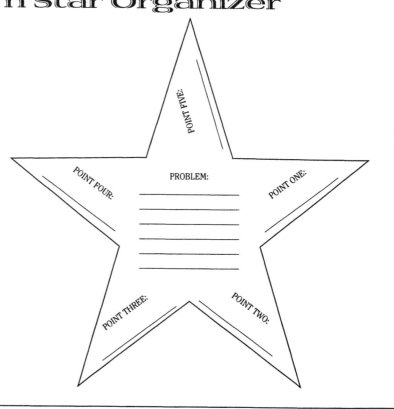

# Sample Graphs

Since it would be difficult, if not impossible, to provide adequate descriptions for the bar graph, line graph, and pictographs to serve as illustrations, these graphs have been shown in model form. They may be easily replicated or modified to meet individual classrooms needs.

See page 44 for reproducible copy.

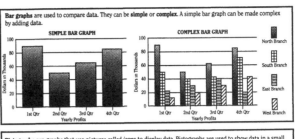

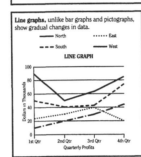

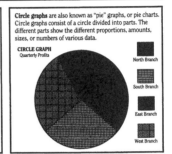

# Step Outline For Writing Math Report

DIRECTIONS: Use the Step Outline at right to record the different tasks required in researching and recording information when preparing a report on a math-related topic.

See page 45 for reproducible copy.

**STEP ONE:** Identifying the Information Required for Report
(What do you want to know?)

**STEP TWO:** Locating the Information
(What resources and tools do you need to obtain information?)

**STEP THREE:** Processing the Information
(How will you organize the information for reporting purposes?)

**STEP FOUR:** Writing and Communicating the Information
(What ideas do you have for the Introduction, Body, and Conclusion of your report?)

# Throw the Dice Organizer

Use each of the dice shapes at right to collect, organize, describe, display, and interpret data that involves the world of statistics. Statistics is a branch of mathematics in which groups of numbers are compared. They are used to compare everything from athletes' achievements to attendance/grade records at school. Be sure to show how one determines the range, median, mode, and mean of a statistics problem described and demonstrated below. Also keep in mind that statistics are often compared in graphs.

See page 46 for reproducible copy.

**Statistics Problem**

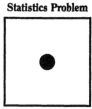

**Finding the Mode**

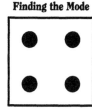

**Finding the Range**

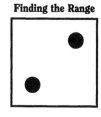

**Finding the Mean**

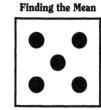

**Finding the Median**

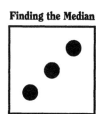

**Graph Representation**

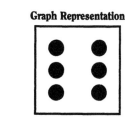

# Training the Mind

Use the Ferris wheel to show the steps in solving a problem related to whole numbers, fractions, decimals, geometry, measurement, or statistics and probability. Write out the problem to be solved on the first seat of the Ferris wheel, the individual steps necessary to solve the problem on the remaining seats (one per seat) and the final answer or solution to the problem on the circle in the center of the Ferris wheel.

See page 47 for reproducible copy.

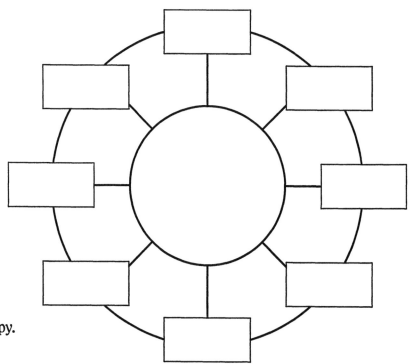

# Venn Diagram

A Venn Diagram consists of three large intersecting circles that are used to compare and contrast three different but related objects, concepts, or events. A Venn Diagram is useful when researching a topic that requires comparison and contrast. As the research is conducted, interrelationships among subtopics will emerge. Areas of commonality may be recorded in the intersecting segments of the circles and differences in the appropriate non-intersecting circles.

See page 48 for reproducible copy.

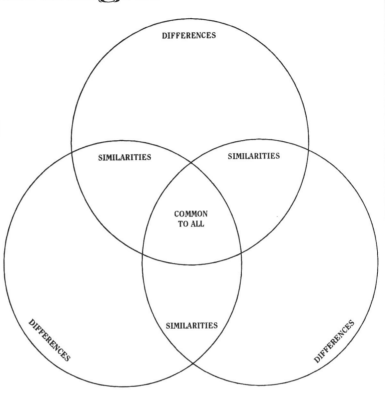

DIFFERENCES

SIMILARITIES          SIMILARITIES

COMMON
TO ALL

DIFFERENCES          SIMILARITIES          DIFFERENCES

# What, So What, Now What?

A *What, So What, Now What?* Chart helps organize one's thinking after working a problem or a series of problems, or completing a project, performance, or portfolio task, or textbook section by requiring the student to reflect back over the information presented.

The *What?* column requires the student to write down a response to the question: *What did I learn from this selection?*

The *So What?* column requires the student to write down a series of responses to the question: *What difference does it make now that I know this?*

The *Now What?* Column asks students to write down some thoughts answering the question: *How can I use this information to make a difference in what I know or can do?*

See page 49 for reproducible copy.

Topic of Study _____

Student's Name _____

| What? | So What? | Now What? |
|-------|----------|-----------|
|       |          |           |

*Standards-Based MATH Graphic Organizers, Rubrics, and Writing Prompts for Middle Grade Students*

# The ABC's of An Important
# Math Topic/Standard

A _____

B _____

C _____

D _____

E _____

F _____

G _____

H _____

I _____

J _____

K _____

L _____

M _____

N _____

O _____

P _____

Q _____

R _____

S _____

T _____

U _____

V _____

W _____

X _____

Y _____

Z _____

*Standards-Based MATH Graphic Organizers, Rubrics,*
*and Writing Prompts for Middle Grade Students*

Copyright ©2001 by Incentive Publications, Inc.
Nashville, TN.

# Biography of a Mathematician

A Biography of: _____

| | |
|---|---|
| Place/Date of Birth | |
| Family History | |
| Early Life | |
| Education | |
| Major Actions | |
| Major Events | |
| Major Influences | |
| Major Contributors | |
| Major Friends | |
| Major Problems | |
| Famous Quotes or Words | |

*Standards-Based MATH Graphic Organizers, Rubrics,
and Writing Prompts for Middle Grade Students*

# Brainstorming Web

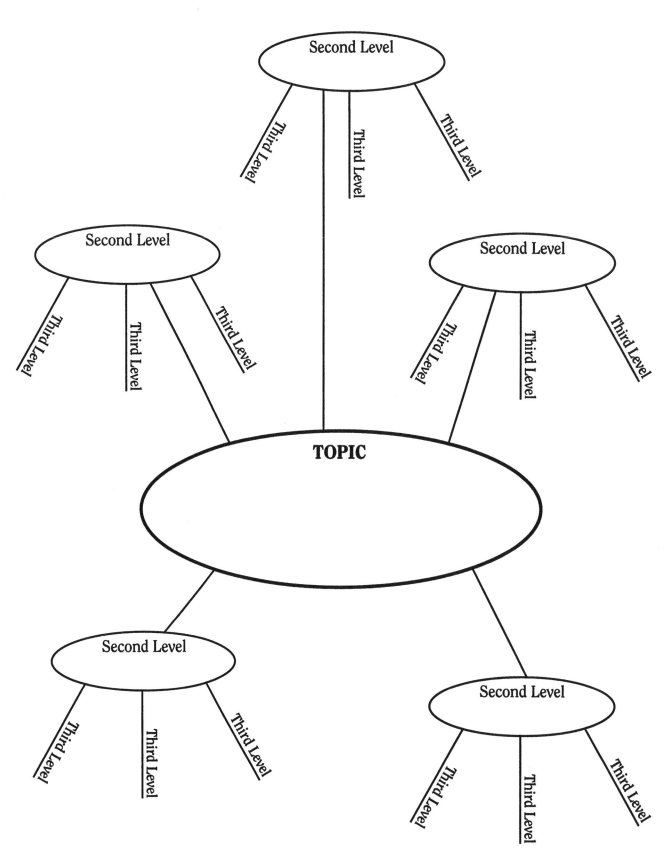

*Standards-Based MATH Graphic Organizers, Rubrics, and Writing Prompts for Middle Grade Students*

# Brochure Building

## Section __

## Section __

## Section __

*Standards-Based MATH Graphic Organizers, Rubrics,*
*and Writing Prompts for Middle Grade Students*

# Calendar Organizer

|  |  |  |  |  |
|--|--|--|--|--|
|  |  |  |  |  |
|  |  |  |  |  |
|  |  |  |  |  |
|  |  |  |  |  |

# Checklist of Questions To Answer When Studying From Math Textbook

What is my purpose for reading this material?
Notes:

What do I already know about this topic?
Notes:

What are the guiding questions I need to be able to answer on this topic?
Notes:

What information is most important here?
Notes:

What questions does this information raise for me?
Notes:

How can I organize this information so I can remember it more easily?
Notes:

How can I visualize or picture this information?
Notes:

What do I want to discuss with my teacher or my class about this information?
Notes:

# Data Graph

Graph for: _____

*Standards-Based MATH Graphic Organizers, Rubrics,*
*and Writing Prompts for Middle Grade Students*

# Decision Chart

## Criteria

**Total Scores**

## Decision to be made

## Alternative Ideas

1.
2.
3.
4.
5.
6.
7.
8.
9.
10.

Scoring of criteria:

| | |
|---|---|
| 3 points | = Great |
| 2 points | = O.K. |
| 1 point | = Not so good |

*Standards-Based MATH Graphic Organizers, Rubrics,
and Writing Prompts for Middle Grade Students*

# Fact and Information Organizer

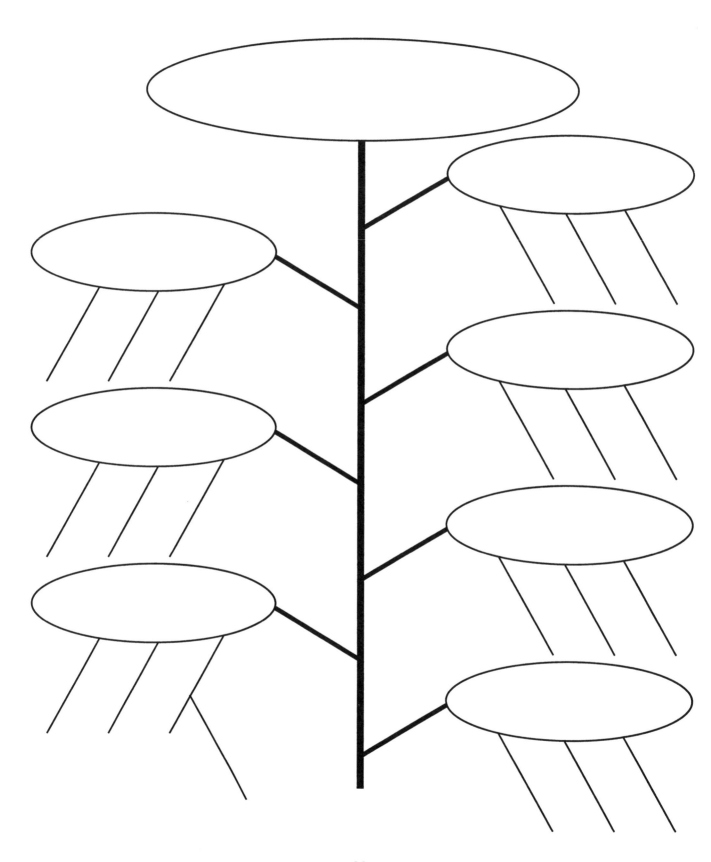

# Filmstrip Organizer

*Standards-Based MATH Graphic Organizers, Rubrics,*
*and Writing Prompts for Middle Grade Students*

# Flowchart

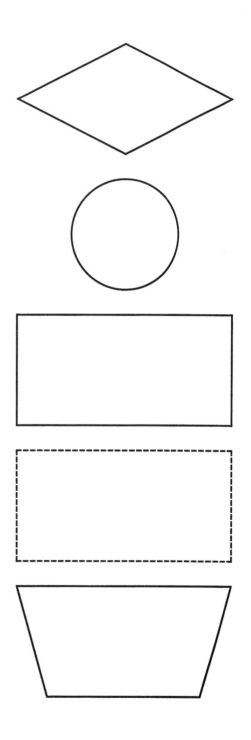
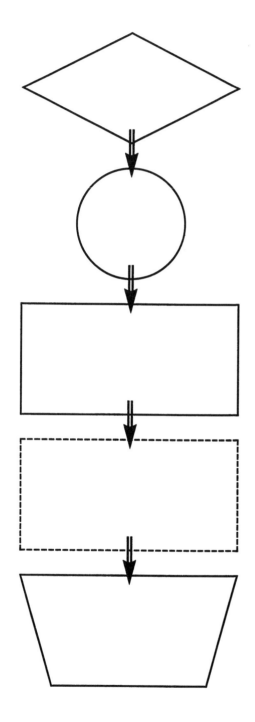

*Standards-Based MATH Graphic Organizers, Rubrics,*
*and Writing Prompts for Middle Grade Students*

# Graph Matrix

Title: _____

*Standards-Based MATH Graphic Organizers, Rubrics,
and Writing Prompts for Middle Grade Students*

# Math Portfolio or Project Plan

Topic:_____ Completion Date:_____

Learning Goals:

Supplies, Resources, and Location:

Project Description:

Steps to Follow:

1.

2.

3.

4.

5.

Assessment Plan:

Student Signature: _____ Date: _____

Teacher Signature: _____ Date: _____

# Math Project Planning Tool

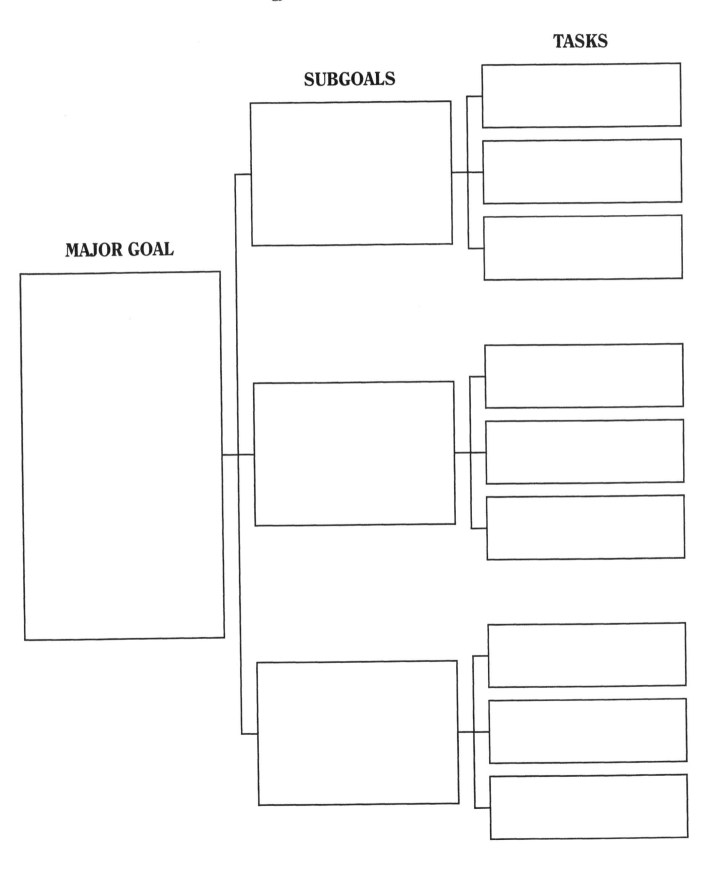

**TASKS**

**SUBGOALS**

**MAJOR GOAL**

*Standards-Based MATH Graphic Organizers, Rubrics,
and Writing Prompts for Middle Grade Students*

# Math Research Study Plan

## PERSONAL PROJECT PLAN

| Title and Description of Study | Beginning Date _____ Completion Date _____ | Format for Study |

**Title and Description of Study**

**Beginning Date**

_____

**Completion Date**

_____

**Format for Study**

**Challenges to be expected and/or questions to answer**

**Resources Needed and Location**

**Method of Evaluation**

Student Signature: _____ Date: _____

Teacher Signature: _____ Date: _____

# Math Vocabulary Learning Ladder

Word or Term: _____

Textbook Sentence: _____

Page: _____ Definition: _____

_____

**5**

Word or Term: _____

Textbook Sentence: _____

Page: _____ Definition: _____

_____

**4**

Word or Term: _____

Textbook Sentence: _____

Page: _____ Definition: _____

_____

**3**

Word or Term: _____

Textbook Sentence: _____

Page: _____ Definition: _____

_____

**2**

Word or Term: _____

Textbook Sentence: _____

Page: _____ Definition: _____

_____

**1**

*Standards-Based MATH Graphic Organizers, Rubrics,
and Writing Prompts for Middle Grade Students*

# Mind Map

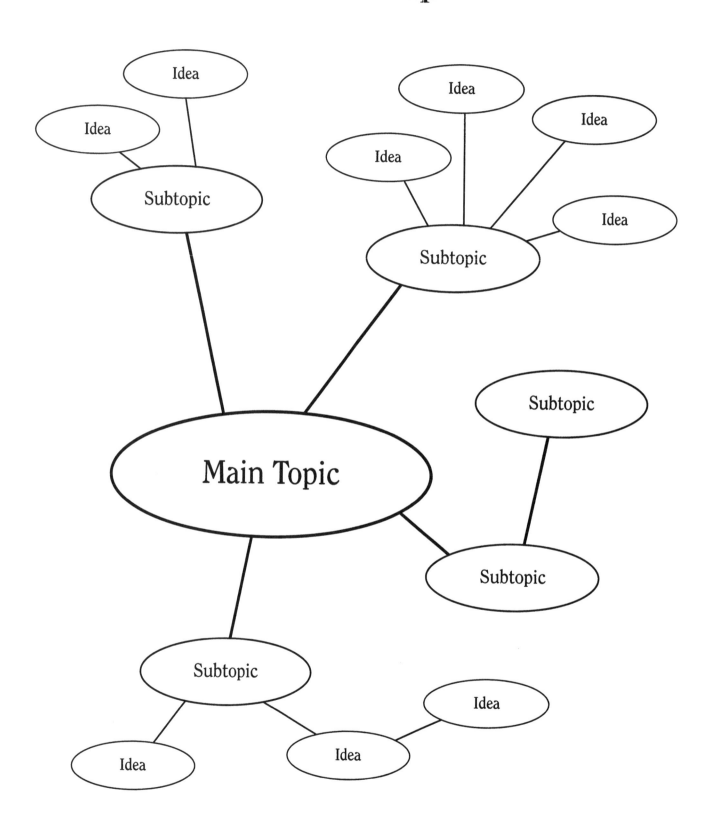

# Prediction Web

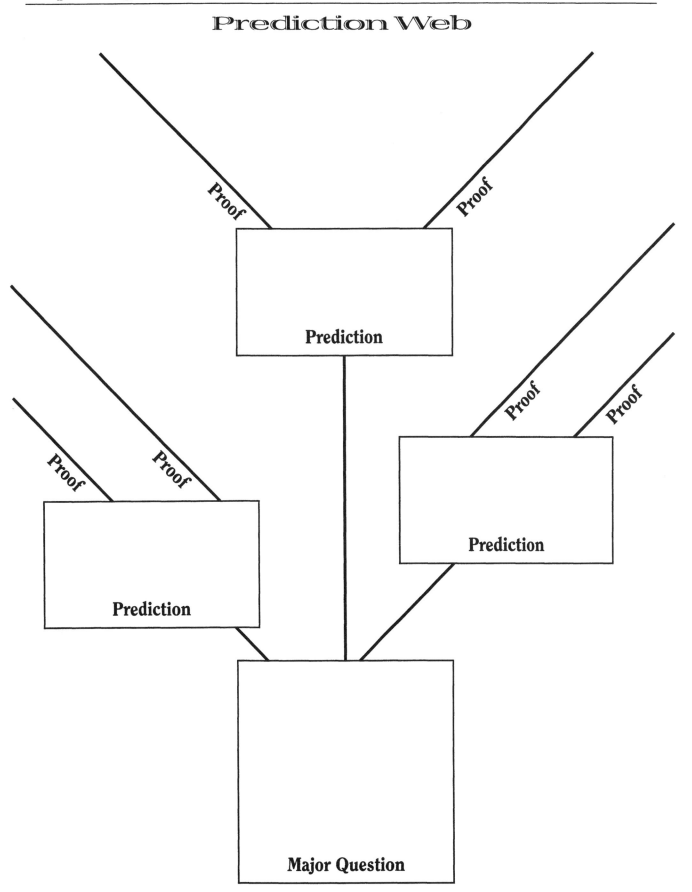

# Problem-Solution Boxes

PROBLEM                                    HOW SOLVED

Standards-Based MATH Graphic Organizers, Rubrics,
and Writing Prompts for Middle Grade Students

# Problem Star Organizer

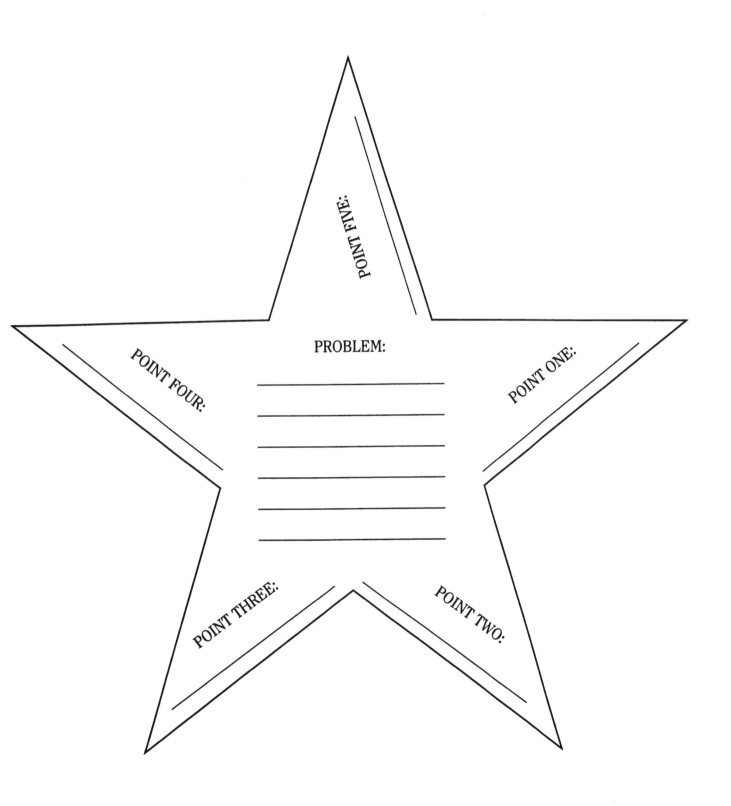

POINT FIVE:

PROBLEM:

POINT FOUR:

POINT ONE:

POINT THREE:

POINT TWO:

*Standards-Based MATH Graphic Organizers, Rubrics,*
*and Writing Prompts for Middle Grade Students*

# Sample Graphs

**Bar graphs** are used to compare data. They can be **simple** or **complex**. A simple bar graph can be made complex by adding data.

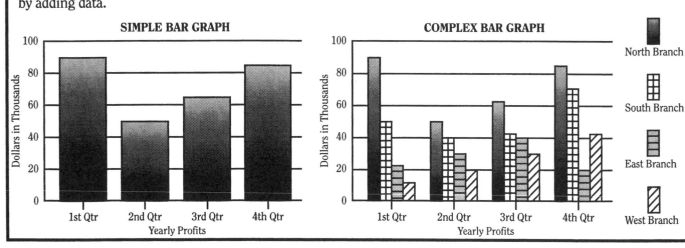

**Pictographs** are graphs that use pictures called *icons* to display data. Pictographs are used to show data in a small space. Pictographs, like bar graphs, compare data. Because pictographs use icons, however, they also include keys, or definitions of the icons.

*Number of pairs of scissors sold*

✂ = 10 pairs of scissors

| | | pairs |
|---|---|---|
| Team A: | ✂ ✂ ✂ ✂ ✂ | 50 pairs |
| Team B: | ✂ ✂ ✂ ✂ ✂ ✂ ✂ ✂ | 75 pairs |
| Team C: | ✂ ✂ ✂ | 30 pairs |

**Line graphs,** unlike bar graphs and pictographs, show gradual changes in data.

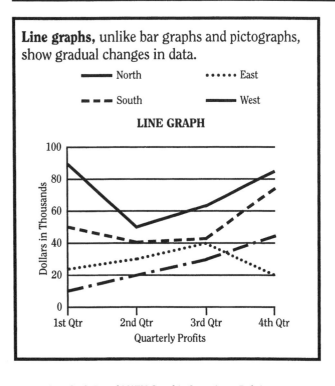

**Circle graphs** are also known as "pie" graphs, or pie charts. Circle graphs consist of a circle divided into parts. The different parts show the different proportions, amounts, sizes, or numbers of various data.

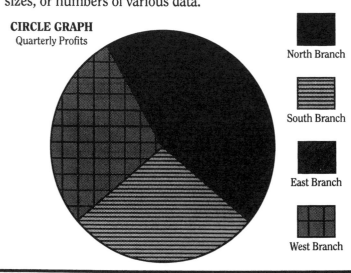

# Step Outline For Writing Math Report

**STEP ONE:** **Identifying the Information Required for Report**
(What do you want to know?)

```



```

**STEP TWO:** **Locating the Information**
(What resources and tools do you need to obtain information?)

```



```

**STEP THREE:** **Processing the Information**
(How will you organize the information for reporting purposes?)

```



```

**STEP FOUR:** **Writing and Communicating the Information**
(What ideas do you have for the Introduction, Body, and Conclusion of your report?)

```



```

*Standards-Based MATH Graphic Organizers, Rubrics,*
*and Writing Prompts for Middle Grade Students*

# Throw the Dice Organizer

### Statistics Problem

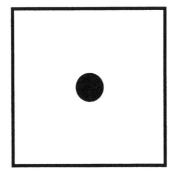

### Finding the Mode

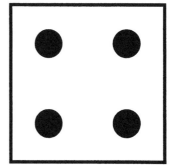

### Finding the Range

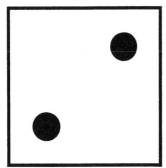

### Finding the Mean

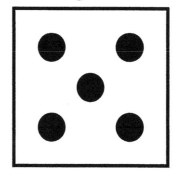

### Finding the Median

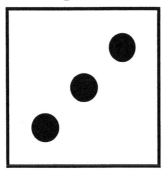

### Graph Representation

# Training the Mind

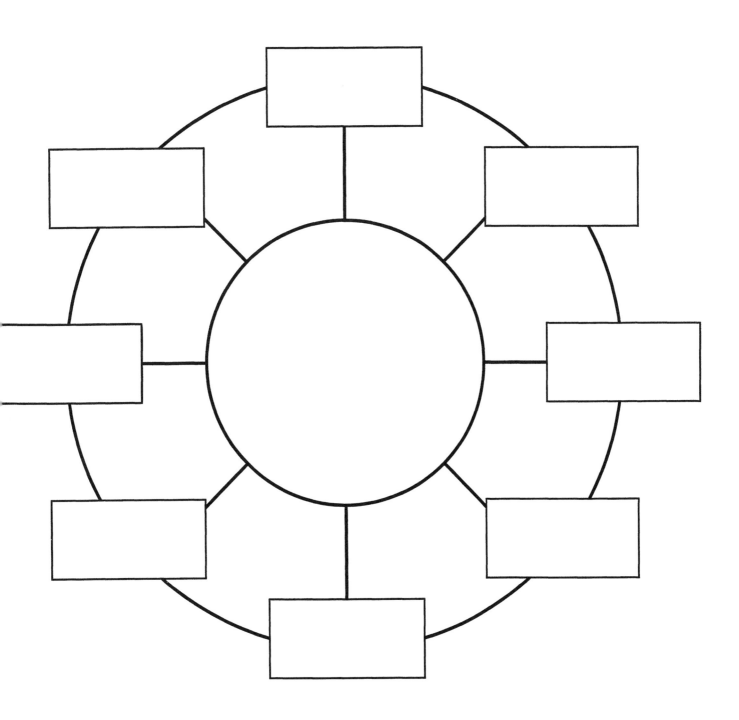

*Standards-Based MATH Graphic Organizers, Rubrics,*
*and Writing Prompts for Middle Grade Students*

# Venn Diagram

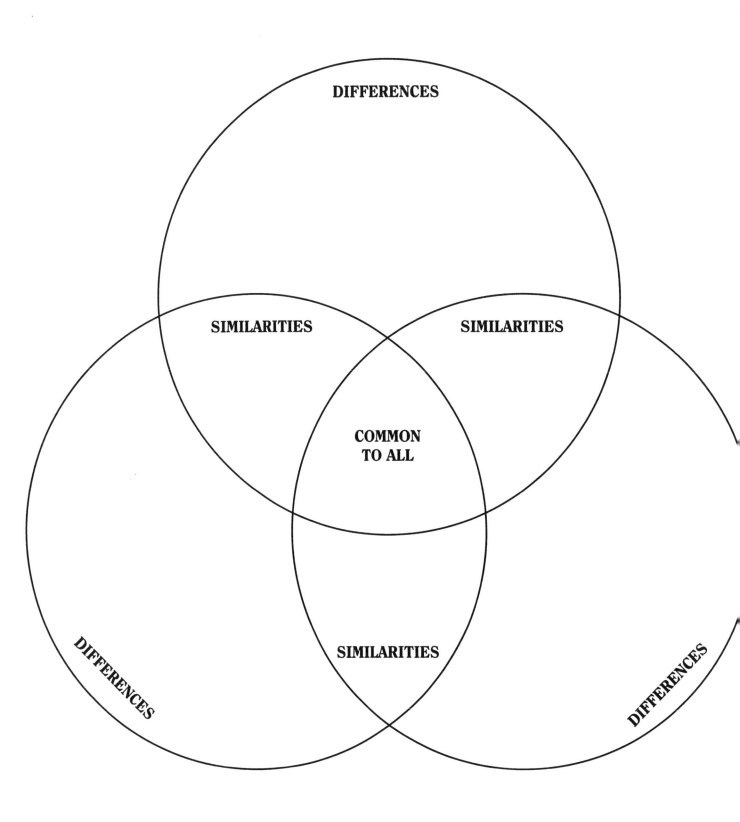

# What, So What, Now What?

Topic of Study_____

Student's Name _____

| What? | So What? | Now What? |
|---|---|---|
|  |  |  |

*Standards-Based MATH Graphic Organizers, Rubrics,
and Writing Prompts for Middle Grade Students*

# Questions for Teachers and Students to Consider About Using Graphic Organizers in the Classroom

1. What is a graphic organizer and what types of graphic organizers are best for my subject area?

2. How can I use graphic organizers to help students collect information, make interpretations, draw conclusions, solve problems, outline plans, and become better reflective thinkers?

3. What graphic organizers can I use that are hierarchical structures with levels and subsets?

4. What graphic organizers can I use that are conceptual structures which take a central idea or concept and branch out from it?

5. What graphic organizers can I use that are sequential structures that focus on the order, chronology, or flow of ideas?

6. What graphic organizers can I use that are cyclical structures, which form a pattern in a circular format?

7. How can I model the use of graphic organizers with my students before introducing them into the instructional process?

8. How can I best model the use of graphic organizers with a wall chart, an overhead projector, or a drawing on the chalkboard?

9. How do graphic organizers show and explain relationships between content and sub-content and how do they in turn relate to the other content areas?

10. How can graphic organizers be considered teaching tools for all types of learners?

11. How can graphic organizers be used as assessment tools to show a student's understanding of a concept and a student's way of thinking about that concept?

12. How do graphic organizers support Bloom's Taxonomy and the Multiple Intelligences?

13. Are graphic organizers best used with individual students or can they be part of cooperative learning group tasks?

14. How can students use graphic organizers to assess their own learning?

*Standards-Based MATH Graphic Organizers, Rubrics, and Writing Prompts for Middle Grade Students*

# Writing Prompts

Compose a short essay discussing the importance of geometry in the field of architecture. Be specific in your ideas.

Write a paragraph to support this statement: number patterns and relationships are all around us. Give examples to support your ideas.

Design a collage composed of rectangles, triangles, squares, and one circle. Name the collage and write a description for a museum catalog.

# GUIDELINES
## FOR USING WRITING PROMPTS

## PURPOSE

A journal is: a collection of ideas, thoughts, and opinions; a place to outline papers and projects, a place to record observations about something read, written or discussed, a record keeping tool, a place in which to write personal reactions or responses, a reference file to help a student monitor individual growth, a way for students to dialogue with teachers and peers, a place for a student to write about a variety of topics, and a place for reflections on learned material.

## FORMATS

Several formats are available for students working with journal writing. Some of the most appealing formats to students and teachers are: special notebooks, segments of audiotapes, file cards, and handmade diaries.

## WRITING TIME

There are several approaches students may use in timing their journal writing. Some may write daily for five minutes, semi-weekly for ten minutes, weekly for fifteen minutes, or write as inspiration strikes.

## STUDENT FEEDBACK

There are several methods, both formal and informal, for sharing students' journal work. Choose one or more of the following to implement in your classroom.
1) Students share their journal entries with their peers.
2) Students read journal entries aloud to the class on a volunteer basis.
3) Journals may be used for "conferencing."
4) Journals are to be taken home and shared with parents or guardians.
5) Students may analyze and answer one of their own journal entries one or more days after the entry was recorded to acknowledge personal changes in perspective.

If you could be any number you wanted to be from 1 to 100, which would you choose to be, and why? Which numbers would you choose for friends and for family members?

_____

_____

_____

_____

_____

_____

_____

_____

_____

_____

Assign a number from 1 to 26 for each letter of the alphabet so that A = 1, B = 2, C = 3, etc. Using this numbering system, determine how much your first and last names are worth. How much are your friends' names worth? What are the most valuable three, four, five, six, seven, eight, nine, and ten words that you can think of? The least valuable three, four, five, six, seven, eight, nine, and ten words that you can think of? What role do consonants and vowels play in the construction of these words?

_____

_____

_____

_____

_____

_____

_____

_____

_____

*Standards-Based MATH Graphic Organizers, Rubrics,
and Writing Prompts for Middle Grade Students*

Write down the numerals from 1 through 9 and answer these questions about them. Which numeral is most artistic? most expressive? most colorful? most useful? most lucky? Give reasons for your choices.

_____

_____

_____

_____

_____

_____

_____

_____

_____

_____

_____

_____

Write a number autobiography telling all about yourself using numbers only. Write this in story or essay form.

_____

_____

_____

_____

_____

_____

_____

_____

_____

_____

_____

_____

_____

*Standards-Based MATH Graphic Organizers, Rubrics, and Writing Prompts for Middle Grade Students*

Create a radio or television commercial that would make other students want to be part of your math class. Share this information with your math teachers.

_____

_____

_____

_____

_____

_____

_____

_____

_____

_____

Spelling mathematical terms can be tricky, and sometimes we make up silly sentences as memory devices. For example, to remember how to spell the word "parallel" we might write something like this: "People ate radishes at little Larry's elite lodge." What funny statements can you write for other geometry-related terms such as "perpendicular," "rhombus," "equilateral," or "tetrahedron"?

_____

_____

_____

_____

_____

_____

_____

_____

_____

Write a paragraph explaining how math is used in your favorite sport. Give specific examples to support your explanations.

_____

_____

_____

_____

_____

_____

_____

_____

_____

_____

_____

Compose a letter of application for a job of your choice that might be a career option in the future. In this letter, explain what position you are applying for, as well as how important your knowledge and expertise in math would be if you were to get the job.

_____

_____

_____

_____

_____

_____

_____

_____

_____

_____

_____

*Standards-Based MATH Graphic Organizers, Rubrics, and Writing Prompts for Middle Grade Students*

Write down a reaction to this statement:
*Without fractions and decimals, our world would be all or nothing.*

_____

_____

_____

_____

_____

_____

_____

_____

_____

_____

_____

Create a comic strip that shows the double meaning for one of these number-related figures of speech:

Her days in this class are numbered!      That lawyer has done a number on you!

He is number one in my book.      After meeting that lady, I have her number.

| | | |
|---|---|---|
| | | |

Design a chart of mathematical facts about a topic that is of special interest to you. Create a series of questions about the information presented that you might ask of others who review your chart.

_____

_____

_____

_____

_____

_____

_____

_____

_____

_____

_____

Organize your thoughts for a debate or discussion on how math is related to both science and music.

_____

_____

_____

_____

_____

_____

_____

_____

_____

_____

_____

*Standards-Based MATH Graphic Organizers, Rubrics, and Writing Prompts for Middle Grade Students*

Write an explanation for each of these statements: How is addition related to multiplication and multiplication related to division? How is division related to subtraction and subtraction related to addition?

_____

_____

_____

_____

_____

_____

_____

_____

_____

_____

Compose a paragraph that illustrates this mathematical observation: "The shape of something has a great deal to do with how we use it."

_____

_____

_____

_____

_____

_____

_____

_____

_____

_____

*Standards-Based MATH Graphic Organizers, Rubrics,*
*and Writing Prompts for Middle Grade Students*

Create a story to explain why the number zero should not feel inferior to the number one hundred. Consider why the numeral zero is so important.

_____

_____

_____

_____

_____

_____

_____

_____

_____

_____

_____

_____

Explain the connections between a line graph, bar graph, and circle graph.

_____

_____

_____

_____

_____

_____

_____

_____

_____

_____

_____

_____

_____

*Standards-Based MATH Graphic Organizers, Rubrics, and Writing Prompts for Middle Grade Students*

Justify to a group of school board members why students should be able to use calculators in math class.

_____

_____

_____

_____

_____

_____

_____

_____

_____

_____

List five ways you use decimals and five ways you use fractions in your everyday life.

_____

_____

_____

_____

_____

_____

_____

_____

_____

_____

_____

Think of at least ten different real life situations where mathematics is needed to solve an important problem.

_____

_____

_____

_____

_____

_____

_____

_____

_____

_____

_____

Make up a word problem for each of the following situations: money and decimals; cooking and fractions; ages and whole numbers; test scores and percentages

_____

_____

_____

_____

_____

_____

_____

_____

_____

_____

_____

*Standards-Based MATH Graphic Organizers, Rubrics, and Writing Prompts for Middle Grade Students*

If you could be a mathematical symbol, which one would you rather be? Consider symbols used in everything from operations on whole numbers to problem solving in geometry.

_____

_____

_____

_____

_____

_____

_____

_____

_____

_____

Compose a letter and a response that might appear in an advice column about a middle school student who is having difficulty with either his math teacher or his math class.

_____

_____

_____

_____

_____

_____

_____

_____

_____

_____

Create a crossword puzzle using only math terms and their definitions. What clues will you give?

_____

_____

_____

_____

_____

_____

_____

_____

_____

_____

_____

Conduct a poll of your math classmates to determine the most popular math activity, or topic studied this year.

_____

_____

_____

_____

_____

_____

_____

_____

_____

_____

_____

_____

*Standards-Based MATH Graphic Organizers, Rubrics, and Writing Prompts for Middle Grade Students*

Would you rather take a test that has 10 questions worth 10 points each, or one with 20 questions worth 5 points each? 25 questions worth 5 points each, or 50 questions worth 2 points each? Explain your reasoning and estimate where you would score the highest.

_____

_____

_____

_____

_____

_____

_____

_____

_____

_____

Estimate how many hours of television the students in your math class watched after school last night and test your prediction.

_____

_____

_____

_____

_____

_____

_____

_____

_____

_____

*Standards-Based MATH Graphic Organizers, Rubrics,*
*and Writing Prompts for Middle Grade Students*

Explain the need for order of operations and describe what happens if the order of operations is not followed. Provide examples in your explanation.

THEME: Number Sense and Numeration: Explain how one's number sense would be helpful in using a calculator to do math calculations for an important project.

_____

_____

_____

_____

_____

_____

_____

_____

_____

Write a short story using as many whole numbers as possible in its content.

THEME: Concepts of Whole Numbers: Write the numbers from one to twenty in a different language, such as French or Spanish.

_____

_____

_____

_____

_____

_____

_____

_____

_____

_____

Standards-Based MATH Graphic Organizers, Rubrics, and Writing Prompts for Middle Grade Students

Design a simple game plan that teaches younger students how to perform whole number operations.

THEME: Whole Number Computation: Write a journal entry your math teacher might write about teaching his/her students whole number operations.

_____

_____

_____

_____

_____

_____

_____

_____

_____

Compose a short essay discussing the importance of geometry in the field of architecture. Be specific in your ideas.

_____

_____

_____

_____

_____

_____

_____

_____

_____

_____

Compare and contrast each of these geometric figures: a rectangle and a square; an oval and a circle: a set of parallel lines and a set of perpendicular lines.

_____

_____

_____

_____

_____

_____

_____

_____

_____

_____

Create an advertisement for a math tool that is used for measurement.

_____

_____

_____

_____

_____

_____

_____

_____

_____

_____

_____

*Standards-Based MATH Graphic Organizers, Rubrics, and Writing Prompts for Middle Grade Students*

Write down as much as you know about the metric system.

_____

_____

_____

_____

_____

_____

_____

_____

_____

_____

_____

Explain the difference between *luck* and *chance*, as you understand it.

_____

_____

_____

_____

_____

_____

_____

_____

_____

_____

Compose a paragraph persuading others that buying a lottery ticket is a low percentage investment.

_____

_____

_____

_____

_____

_____

_____

_____

_____

_____

_____

Explain in three different ways what is meant when we say fractions are equivalent.

_____

_____

_____

_____

_____

_____

_____

_____

_____

_____

_____

*Standards-Based MATH Graphic Organizers, Rubrics, and Writing Prompts for Middle Grade Students*

Plan a theme party around the topic of "Fraction Action." Describe what you would eat and do, how you would decorate, and who you would invite.

_____

_____

_____

_____

_____

_____

_____

_____

_____

_____

_____

Create a mini-booklet to teach the basics of decimals. Include both illustrations and explanations.

_____

_____

_____

_____

_____

_____

_____

_____

_____

_____

_____

Think of three activities that you could do to teach the concept of decimals to students with limited English proficiency.

_____

_____

_____

_____

_____

_____

_____

_____

_____

_____

_____

Write a paragraph to support this statement: number patterns and relationships are all around us. Give examples to support your ideas.

_____

_____

_____

_____

_____

_____

_____

_____

_____

_____

_____

*Standards-Based MATH Graphic Organizers, Rubrics, and Writing Prompts for Middle Grade Students*

Compose a letter to a friend that you would like to work with on a math project. Explain what kind of project you would like to do and how your relationship with one another might help produce a quality product.

_____

_____

_____

_____

_____

_____

_____

_____

_____

_____

_____

Design a collage composed of rectangles, triangles, squares, and one circle. Name the collage and write a description for a museum catalog.

_____

_____

_____

_____

_____

_____

_____

_____

_____

_____

_____

Make up a jump rope jingle using addition and subtraction facts.

_____

_____

_____

_____

_____

_____

_____

_____

_____

_____

_____

Thumb through your math book for the purpose of evaluating its usability for its intended purpose. Consider the readability of the text, the book's format and organization, the quality of graphics, vocabulary use, interest level of the assignments, and ease or difficulty of access to basic math facts. Write an objective critique of the book, compare your critique with ones written by your classmates.

_____

_____

_____

_____

_____

_____

_____

_____

*Standards-Based MATH Graphic Organizers, Rubrics, and Writing Prompts for Middle Grade Students*

Make a list of four sources of information that you could turn to for help with your math assignments right now. Rank order your list in terms of usefulness. Make a star beside each one you have used within the past 60 days.

_____

_____

_____

_____

_____

_____

_____

_____

_____

_____

_____

Write a letter to a student your age living in another country describing the math program in your grade in your school. Tell the student how you feel about its expectancies for study and how you plan to go about achieving them.

_____

_____

_____

_____

_____

_____

_____

_____

_____

_____

_____

*Standards-Based MATH Graphic Organizers, Rubrics,
and Writing Prompts for Middle Grade Students*

Complete the sentences below as honestly as you can. Then use one of the completed sentences as a springboard for a paragraph or brief essay expressing your true feelings about the math program in your school. Try to make references to things you like and supply specific suggestions for changes if you feel they are in order.

I think our math classes are _____ .

I like math better than _____ , but less than _____ .

If I were in charge of the math program for my grade, I would _____

_____ .

_____

_____

_____

_____

_____

_____

_____

Design a learning poster to teach a new student in your math class, whose language is different from your own, how to make use of the computers available to your class. Try to make the directions as specific and as easy to follow as possible. Remember you will need to limit your use of words and rely heavily on graphics.

_____

_____

_____

_____

_____

_____

_____

_____

_____

_____

_____

Standards-Based MATH Graphic Organizers, Rubrics, and Writing Prompts for Middle Grade Students

# Rubrics

Rubric: _____

## Assessment Rubric for
## Circle, Bar, or Line Graph

★    ★ ★    ★ ★ ★    ★ ★ ★ ★

**Rating Scale:**

1. The graph conveys the important and intended information (data) clearly.  Rating _____

2. The graph conveys the important and intended information (data) accurately.  Rating _____

3. The graph conveys the important and intended information (data) visually.  Rating _____

4. The graph conveys the important and intended information (data) creatively.  Rating _____

5. The graph conveys the important information (data) correctly for graph construction.

Comments by Student: _____
_____
Signed _____

Comments by Teacher: _____
_____
Signed _____

Rubric:

## Assessment Rubric for Constructing
## A Flowchart or Spreadsheet

**Rating Scale:**  ①  ②  ③

**1. Appropriateness of Topic Selected for Flowchart or Spreadsheet**

My topic was chosen because it lends itself to the flowchart/spreadsheet format.  ① ② ③

**2. Quality of Information/Data Presented in Flowchart or Spreadsheet**

My flowchart/spreadsheet conveys important information on my topic. It records key data and/or processes with clarity and precision.

**3. Accuracy in Design/Construction of Flowchart**

My flowchart/spreadsheet represents the correct symbols, figures, and layout necessary for its design/construction.

**4. Interests and Creativity**

My flowchart/spreadsheet generates interest on the part of the reader because it records information visually in an original and effective way.

Comments by Student: _____
_____
Signed _____

Comments by Teacher: _____
_____
Signed _____

Rubric: _____

## Assessment Rubric for
## Participation in Group Discussion

Name: _____
Topic of Discussion: _____  Date: _____
Questions to Consider: _____
_____

**Rating Scale:**  ☺  ☺  ☹

1. I took an active part in the discussion.

2. I did not participate too much or too little.  Rating _____

3. I listened attentively to the ideas of others.  Rating _____

4. I thought about my comments before I shared them with others.  Rating _____

5. I prepared adequately for the discussion topic.  Rating _____

6. I respected the ideas of my classmates.  Rating _____

7. I made my points promptly and clearly.  Rating _____

8. I encouraged others to join the discussion.  Rating _____

9. I showed patience with others who had difficulty expressing their ideas.  Rating _____

10. I exhibited appropriate risk-taking in expressing my thoughts.  Rating _____

The best thing about today's discussion for me was .

Next time, I plan to . . .

# Assessment Checklist for Decimals, Ratios, and Percentages

**Rating Scale:** ✔+      ✔      ✔−

---

**1. Student is able to identify and define these terms:**

| | | | |
|---|---|---|---|
| Decimal fraction | Rating: _____ | Ratios | Rating: _____ |
| Repeating decimal | Rating: _____ | Percentages | Rating: _____ |
| Place value | Rating: _____ | Proportion | Rating: _____ |
| Decimal/Fraction equivalents | Rating: _____ | | |

---

**2. Student is able to add decimals.**      Rating: _____

---

**3. Student is able to subtract decimals.**      Rating: _____

---

**4. Student is able to multiply decimals.**      Rating: _____

---

**5. Student is able to divide decimals.**      Rating: _____

---

**6. Student is able to write decimal fractions or ratios as percentages.**      Rating: _____

---

**7. Student is able to calculate ratios and percentages.**      Rating: _____

---

**8. Student is able to give real world applications of decimals, ratios, and percentages.**      Rating: _____

SAMPLES OF MY ABILITY TO PERFORM DECIMAL OPERATIONS/CALCULATIONS:

_____

_____

_____

_____

# Assessment Checklist for Fractions

**Rating Scale:**      ✔+                    ✔                    ✔−

---

### 1. Student is able to identify and define these terms:

Numerator          Rating: _____

Denominator        Rating: _____      Common denominators    Rating: _____

Proper fraction    Rating: _____      Equivalent fraction    Rating: _____

Mixed numeral      Rating: _____      Least common multiple  Rating: _____

Improper fraction  Rating: _____

---

### 2. Student is able to add fractions:

With common denominators          Rating: _____

With mixed numerals               Rating: _____

---

### 3. Student is able to subtract fractions:

With common denominators          Rating: _____

With mixed numerals               Rating: _____

---

### 4. Student is able to multiply fractions:

By a whole number                 Rating: _____

One fraction by another fraction  Rating: _____

Mixed numerals by fractions       Rating: _____

---

### 5. Student is able to divide fractions:

By a whole number                     Rating: _____

A whole number by a fraction          Rating: _____

A fraction by another fraction        Rating: _____

A mixed numeral by another mixed numeral   Rating: _____

---

### 6. Student is able to change a fraction to a decimal fraction.

Rating: _____

---

*Standards-Based MATH Graphic Organizers, Rubrics,
and Writing Prompts for Middle Grade Students*

# Assessment Checklist for Geometry

**Rating Scale:**      ✔+        ✔        ✔−

---

**1. Student is able to identify, define, write symbols for, and construct each of these terms/concepts:**

| | | | |
|---|---|---|---|
| Points | Rating: _____ | Parallel lines | Rating: _____ |
| Lines | Rating: _____ | Intersecting lines | Rating: _____ |
| Line Segments | Rating: _____ | Perpendicular lines | Rating: _____ |
| Rays | Rating: _____ | Planes | Rating: _____ |

---

**2. Student is able to identify, define, write symbols for, and construct each of these terms/concepts:**

| | | | |
|---|---|---|---|
| Angles | Rating: _____ | Right angles | Rating: _____ |
| Vertex | Rating: _____ | Reflex angles | Rating: _____ |
| Acute angles | Rating: _____ | Complementary angles | Rating: _____ |
| Obtuse angles | Rating: _____ | Supplementary angles | Rating: _____ |

---

**3. Student is able to identify, define, and construct each of these terms/concepts:**

| | |
|---|---|
| Polygons | Rating: _____ |
| Concave polygons | Rating: _____ |
| Convex polygons | Rating: _____ |
| Regular and irregular polygons | Rating: _____ |

---

**4. Student is able to identify, define, and construct each of these terms/concepts:**

| | | | |
|---|---|---|---|
| Triangles | Rating: _____ | Isosceles triangles | Rating: _____ |
| Right triangles | Rating: _____ | Scalene triangles | Rating: _____ |
| | | Equilateral triangles | Rating: _____ |

---

**5. Student is able to identify, define, write symbols for, and construct each of these terms/concepts:**

| | | | |
|---|---|---|---|
| Quadrilaterals | Rating: _____ | Rhombuses | Rating: _____ |
| Parallelograms | Rating: _____ | Pentagons | Rating: _____ |
| Trapezoids | Rating: _____ | Hexagons | Rating: _____ |
| Squares | Rating: _____ | Octagons | Rating: _____ |
| Rectangles | Rating: _____ | | |

---

80

# Assessment Checklist for Geometry
## (continued)

**Rating Scale:** ✔+         ✔         ✔−

---

**6. Student is able to identify, define, write symbols for, and construct each of these terms/concepts:**

| | | | |
|---|---|---|---|
| Circles | Rating: _____ | Diameter | Rating: _____ |
| Radius | Rating: _____ | Circumference | Rating: _____ |

---

**7. Student is able to identify, define, write symbols for, and construct each of these terms/concepts:**

Symmetry      Rating: _____

Congruence      Rating: _____

Similarity      Rating: _____

---

**8. Student is able to identify, define, and construct each of these terms/concepts:**

| | | | |
|---|---|---|---|
| Solids or space figures | Rating: _____ | Spheres | Rating: _____ |
| Cubes | Rating: _____ | Cylinders | Rating: _____ |
| Prisms | Rating: _____ | Cones | Rating: _____ |
| Pyramids | Rating: _____ | | |

---

Comments by Student: _____

_____

_____

_____

Signed _____ Date _____

Comments by Teacher: _____

_____

_____

_____

Signed _____ Date _____

*Standards-Based MATH Graphic Organizers, Rubrics,
and Writing Prompts for Middle Grade Students*

# Assessment Checklist for Measuring Temperature and Time

**Rating Scale:** ✔+      ✔      ✔−

---

1. **Student is able to identify and define these terms:**

   Fahrenheit scale    Rating: _____

   Centigrade or Celsius scale    Rating: _____

   Absolute zero    Rating: _____

---

2. **Student is able to identify Fahrenheit/Centigrade equivalents.**    Rating: _____

---

3. **Student is able to convert from Fahrenheit to centigrade scale.**    Rating: _____

---

4. **Student is able to convert from centigrade to Fahrenheit scale.**    Rating: _____

---

5. **Student is able to identify and define these ancient and modern calendars:**

   The Babylonian Calendar    Rating: _____

   The Egyptian Calendar    Rating: _____

   The Chinese Calendar    Rating: _____

   The Hebrew Calendar    Rating: _____

   Christian Calendars    Rating: _____

   The Hindu Calendar    Rating: _____

   The Muslim Calendar    Rating: _____

   The Roman Calendar    Rating: _____

   The Julian Calendar    Rating: _____

   The Gregorian Calendar    Rating: _____

---

6. **Student is able to explain the concepts of day, month, and year.**    Rating: _____

Standards-Based MATH Graphic Organizers, Rubrics, and Writing Prompts for Middle Grade Students

# Assessment Checklist for Measuring Temperature and Time (continued)

**Rating Scale:**     ✔+          ✔          ✔−

---

**7. Student is able to identify and define these time concepts:**

Standard time                                              Rating: _____

Daylight Savings time                                      Rating: _____

Military time                                              Rating: _____

---

**8. Student is able to identify and briefly describe these early and modern timepieces:**

Shadow sticks                                              Rating: _____

Sundials                                                   Rating: _____

Water clocks                                               Rating: _____

Lamps and candle clocks                                    Rating: _____

Sandglasses                                                Rating: _____

Mechanical and quartz clocks                               Rating: _____

Digital clock                                              Rating: _____

---

Comments by Student: _____

_____

_____

_____

          Signed _____ Date _____

Comments by Teacher: _____

_____

_____

_____

          Signed _____ Date _____

# Assessment Checklist for Measuring Length and Distance

**Rating Scale:**         ✔+                    ✔                    ✔—

---

1. **Student is able to identify and define these early methods of measuring length and distance:**

   | | | | |
   |---|---|---|---|
   | Digit | Rating: _____ | Fathom | Rating: _____ |
   | Span | Rating: _____ | Hand | Rating: _____ |
   | Cubit | Rating: _____ | Foot | Rating: _____ |
   | Pace | Rating: _____ | Rod | Rating: _____ |

2. **Student is able to identify and define these English System or standards for measuring length and their corresponding abbreviations and equivalents:**

   | | | | |
   |---|---|---|---|
   | Inch | Rating: _____ | Furlong | Rating: _____ |
   | Foot | Rating: _____ | Mile | Rating: _____ |
   | Yard | Rating: _____ | League | Rating: _____ |
   | Rod | Rating: _____ | | |

3. **Student is able to identify and define the Metric System or standards for measuring length and their corresponding abbreviations, metric equivalents, and English equivalents:**

   | | | | |
   |---|---|---|---|
   | Millimeter | Rating: _____ | Decameter | Rating: _____ |
   | Centimeter | Rating: _____ | Hectometer | Rating: _____ |
   | Decimeter | Rating: _____ | Kilometer | Rating: _____ |
   | Meter | Rating: _____ | | |

4. **Student is able to identify and describe how measurement at sea is different from measurement on land using fathoms and nautical miles rather than miles and kilometers.**          Rating: _____

5. **Student is able to identify and define these Space Age Measures:**

   | | |
   |---|---|
   | Longitude and lines of longitude | Rating: _____ |
   | Latitude and lines of latitude | Rating: _____ |
   | International Date Line | Rating: _____ |
   | Light years | Rating: _____ |
   | Prime meridian | Rating: _____ |

# Assessment Checklist for Measuring Weight

**Rating Scale:**     ✔+                    ✔                    ✔−

---

1. **Student is able to identify and define these Avoirdupois Weight concepts as well as their abbreviations and equivalents:**

   | | | | |
   |---|---|---|---|
   | Gain | Rating: _____ | Ton | Rating: _____ |
   | Dram | Rating: _____ | Hundredweight | Rating: _____ |
   | Ounce | Rating: _____ | Long hundredweight | Rating: _____ |
   | Pound | Rating: _____ | Gross | Rating: _____ |

2. **Student is able to identify and define these Metric Weight concepts as well as their abbreviations, metric equivalents, and English equivalents:**

   | | | | |
   |---|---|---|---|
   | Gram | Rating: _____ | Decagram | Rating: _____ |
   | Milligram | Rating: _____ | Hectogram | Rating: _____ |
   | Centigram | Rating: _____ | Kilogram | Rating: _____ |
   | Decigram | Rating: _____ | Metric ton | Rating: _____ |

3. **Student is able to give real world examples and applications of when Avoirdupois Weights are commonly used.**     Rating: _____

4. **Student is able to give real world examples and applications of when Metric Weights are commonly used.**     Rating: _____

---

Comments by Student: _____

_____

_____

_____

Signed _____ Date _____

Comments by Teacher: _____

_____

_____

_____

Signed _____ Date _____

*Standards-Based MATH Graphic Organizers, Rubrics,*
*and Writing Prompts for Middle Grade Students*

# Assessment Checklist for Measuring Perimeter, Area, and Volume of Geometric Shapes

**Rating Scale:**    ✔+        ✔        ✔−

1. **Student is able to demonstrate understanding of the concept of "pi" and its symbol.**          Rating: _____

2. **Student is able to write the formula and perform the calculation for the perimeters of these two-dimensional figures or spaces:**

   Perimeter of a square                          Rating: _____

   Perimeter of a triangle                        Rating: _____

   Perimeter of a rhombus                         Rating: _____

   Perimeter of an irregular polygon              Rating: _____

   Perimeter of a circle                          Rating: _____

3. **Student is able to write the formula and perform the calculation for the areas of these two-dimensional figures or spaces:**

   Area of a square                               Rating: _____

   Area of a triangle                             Rating: _____

   Area of a rectangle                            Rating: _____

   Area of a parallelogram                        Rating: _____

   Area of a rhombus                              Rating: _____

   Area of a circle                               Rating: _____

4. **Student is able to write the formula and perform the calculation for the volumes in three-dimensional shapes:**

   Volume of a rectangular prism                  Rating: _____

   Volume of a cube                               Rating: _____

   Volume of a pyramid                            Rating: _____

   Volume of a cylinder                           Rating: _____

   Volume of a cone                               Rating: _____

   Volume of a sphere                             Rating: _____

# Assessment Checklist for Whole Number Operations

**Rating Scale:**      Yes      Somewhat      No

| | |
|---|---|
| **1.** Student knows and understands the properties of addition. | Yes      No      Somewhat |
| **2.** Student knows and understands the properties of subtraction. | Yes      No      Somewhat |
| **3.** Student knows and understands the properties of multiplication. | Yes      No      Somewhat |
| **4.** Student knows and understands the properties of division. | Yes      No      Somewhat |
| **5.** Student knows and understands when and how to use the various operations. | Yes      No      Somewhat |
| **6.** Student knows and understands how the operations relate to one another. | Yes      No      Somewhat |
| **7.** Student knows and understands how to compute with whole numbers. | Yes      No      Somewhat |

Special strengths of student when working with whole numbers:

_____

_____

_____

Areas of whole number concepts that need further work:

_____

_____

_____

*Standards-Based MATH Graphic Organizers, Rubrics, and Writing Prompts for Middle Grade Students*

# Assessment for Math
# As Communication

**Rating Scale:**  ❤ ❤ ❤          ❤ ❤              ❤

                **BEST**        **NEXT BEST**      **KEEP WORKING ON IT**

| | | |
|---|---|---|
| **1.** Student uses math signs correctly and labels answers appropriately | ❤ ❤ ❤  ❤ ❤ | ❤ |
| **2.** Student applies variety of appropriate strategies and communicates why choices were made. | ❤ ❤ ❤  ❤ ❤ | ❤ |
| **3.** Student demonstrates flexibility in thinking and explains the logic behind that thinking. | ❤ ❤ ❤  ❤ ❤ | ❤ |
| **4.** Student connects mathematics to real world situations and describes conditions and/or applications accurately. | ❤ ❤ ❤  ❤ ❤ | ❤ |
| **5.** Student applies an advanced level of appropriate math language. | ❤ ❤ ❤  ❤ ❤ | ❤ |
| **6.** Student consistently explains process and solution clearly, confidently, and independently. | ❤ ❤ ❤  ❤ ❤ | ❤ |
| **7.** Student understands that math has a language of its own. | ❤ ❤ ❤  ❤ ❤ | ❤ |

Comments by Student: _____

_____

_____

        Signed _____ Date _____

Comments by Teacher: _____

_____

_____

        Signed _____ Date _____

# Assessment Rubric for
# Circle, Bar, or Line Graph

**Rating Scale:**  ★    ★ ★    ★ ★ ★    ★ ★ ★ ★

1. The graph conveys the important and intended information (data) clearly.

   Rating: _____

2. The graph conveys the important and intended information (data) accurately.

   Rating: _____

3. The graph conveys the important and intended information (data) visually.

   Rating: _____

4. The graph conveys the important and intended information (data) creatively.

   Rating: _____

5. The graph conveys the important and intended information (data) correctly in terms of guidelines for graph construction.

   Rating: _____

Comments by Student: _____

_____

_____

Signed _____ Date _____


Comments by Teacher: _____

_____

_____

Signed _____ Date _____

*Standards-Based MATH Graphic Organizers, Rubrics,
and Writing Prompts for Middle Grade Students*

# Assessment Rubric for Constructing A Flowchart or Spreadsheet

**Rating Scale:**    ①    ②    ③

---

### 1. Appropriateness of Topic Selected for Flowchart or Spreadsheet

My topic was chosen because it lends itself
to the flowchart/spreadsheet format.    ①  ②  ③

---

### 2. Quality of Information/Data Presented in Flowchart or Spreadsheet

My flowchart/spreadsheet conveys important
information on my topic. It records key data
and/or processes with clarity and precision.    ①  ②  ③

---

### 3. Accuracy in Design/Construction of Flowchart or Spreadsheet

My flowchart/spreadsheet represents the
correct symbols, figures, and layout
necessary for its design/construction.    ①  ②  ③

---

### 4. Interests and Creativity

My flowchart/spreadsheet generates interest on the
part of the reader because it records information
visually in an original and effective way.    ①  ②  ③

---

Comments by Student: _____

_____

_____

Signed _____ Date _____

Comments by Teacher: _____

_____

_____

Signed _____ Date _____

# Assessment Rubric for
# Figuring Averages and Medians

**Rating Scale:**     **Wow!**                    **OK**                    **Not Yet**

| | | | |
|---|---|---|---|
| 1. Student is able to identify and define the concepts of *average, mean, median,* and *mode*. | Wow! | OK | Not Yet |
| 2. Student is able to compute the average or mean of a list of numbers. | Wow! | OK | Not Yet |
| 3. Student is able to identify the median in a series of numbers. | Wow! | OK | Not Yet |
| 4. Student is able to identify the mode in a series of numbers. | Wow! | OK | Not Yet |
| 5. Student is able to give real world examples of when and why it is important to be able to find the mean, median, and mode of a series of numbers. | Wow! | OK | Not Yet |
| 6. Student is able to explain why averages and medians are important in the branches of math called probability and statistics. | Wow! | OK | Not Yet |

Comments by Student: _____

_____

_____

_____

Signed _____ Date _____

Comments by Teacher: _____

_____

_____

_____

Signed _____ Date _____

*Standards-Based MATH Graphic Organizers, Rubrics,
and Writing Prompts for Middle Grade Students*

# Assessment Rubric for
# Making Mathematical Connections

**Rating Scale:**      WELL DONE      MEDIUM      NEEDS MORE

| | | | |
|---|---|---|---|
| 1. Quality of my examples on how math is used in science | Well Done | Medium | Needs More |
| 2. Quality of my examples on how math is used in social studies | Well Done | Medium | Needs More |
| 3. Quality of my examples on how math is used in careers | Well Done | Medium | Needs More |
| 4. Quality of my examples on how math is used in art & architecture | Well Done | Medium | Needs More |
| 5. Quality of my examples on how math is used in music | Well Done | Medium | Needs More |
| 6. Quality of my examples on how math is used in physical education | Well Done | Medium | Needs More |
| 7. Quality of my examples on how math is used in health | Well Done | Medium | Needs More |
| 8. Quality of my examples on how math is used in language arts | Well Done | Medium | Needs More |

# Assessment Rubric for Math Project

**Rating Scale:** | **H** | **S** | **L**
To High Degree | Satisfactory Degree | Limited Degree

**My project shows that:**

| | |
|---|---|
| 1. I chose an appropriate math topic for my project. | Rating: _____ |
| 2. I did adequate research on my math topic. | Rating: _____ |
| 3. I understood my math topic well. | Rating: _____ |
| 4. I chose a good project format for my math topic. | Rating: _____ |
| 5. I developed a comprehensive outline and time line for completing my project. | Rating: _____ |
| 6. I was able to problem solve while working on my project. | Rating: _____ |
| 7. I completed my project on time. | Rating: _____ |
| 8. I felt good about the quality of my final project. | Rating: _____ |
| 9. Others have given me good input and feedback on my project. | Rating: _____ |
| 10. I enjoyed doing this project. | Rating: _____ |

Comments by Student: _____

_____

Signed _____ Date _____

Comments by Teacher: _____

_____

Signed _____ Date _____

*Standards-Based MATH Graphic Organizers, Rubrics,
and Writing Prompts for Middle Grade Students*

# Assessment Rubric for
# My Number Autobiography

**Rating Scale:**    4 = EXCELLENT    3 = GOOD    2 = FAIR    1 = POOR

## 1. Quality of number autobiography format

The autobiography report conveys information about me
that includes many numbers of importance in my life.
These are summarized in at least ten paragraphs.    **Rating:** _____

## 2. Quality of numbers selected

The numbers considered and selected for my autobiography are key
to understanding who I am, are relevant to important events in my life,
and are varied in their references. The numerical breakdown of
information in my autobiography makes logical sense and
is organized well to cover my life up to this point in time.    **Rating:** _____

## 3. Grammar

The grammar and spelling in my autobiography is good.    **Rating:** _____

## 4. Interest

The autobiography is attractive, entertaining,
and enjoyable to read.    **Rating:** _____

## 5. Graphics/Creativity

The autobiography contains high quality graphics and images where
appropriate to enhance its eye appeal and its information.    **Rating:** _____

# Assessment Rubric for Oral Presentation

**Rating Scale:**  D = 1  C = 2  B = 3  A = 4

1. Clear, accurate, strong math vocabulary  Rating: _____

2. Clear focus and precise information on math topic  Rating: _____

3. Unique presentation of math concepts  Rating: _____

4. Well-organized in delivery of math ideas and explanations  Rating: _____

5. Time used well in both preparation and delivery of math content  Rating: _____

6. Speaking voice and body language were positive and direct when discussing math information  Rating: _____

7. Creative integration of math facts, descriptions, and examples  Rating: _____

8. Evidence of pride and enjoyment in math-oriented performance  Rating: _____

Comments by Teacher: _____

_____

_____

_____

_____

_____

# Assessment Rubric for
# Participation in Group Discussion

Name: _____ Date: _____

Topic of Discussion: _____

Questions to Consider: _____

_____

_____

**Rating Scale:**  ☺           ☺           ☹

| | |
|---|---|
| **1. I took an active part in the discussion.** | Rating: _____ |
| **2. I did not participate too much or too little.** | Rating: _____ |
| **3. I listened attentively to the ideas of others.** | Rating: _____ |
| **4. I thought about my comments before I shared them with others.** | Rating: _____ |
| **5. I prepared adequately for the discussion topic.** | Rating: _____ |
| **6. I respected the ideas of my classmates.** | Rating: _____ |
| **7. I made my points promptly and clearly.** | Rating: _____ |
| **8. I encouraged others to join the discussion.** | Rating: _____ |
| **9. I showed patience with others who had difficulty expressing their ideas.** | Rating: _____ |
| **10. I exhibited appropriate risk-taking in expressing my thoughts.** | Rating: _____ |

The best thing about today's discussion for me was . . .

_____

Next time, I plan to . . .

_____

# Assessment Rubric for Problem-Solving Skills

| Rating Scale: | **+** | **O** | **—** |
|---|---|---|---|
| | WOW! | OK | BOO-HOO! |

1. I can solve word problems
   by recognizing clue words such as
   "increased by" for addition,
   "fewer" for subtraction,
   "product of" for multiplication,
   and "part" for division.                    Rating: _____

2. I can solve word problems
   by circling clue words,
   boxing important information,
   and crossing out unimportant information.    Rating: _____

3. I can solve word problems
   by making lists and/or charts of information.   Rating: _____

4. I can solve word problems
   by finding a pattern.                        Rating: _____

5. I can solve word problems
   by drawing a picture.                        Rating: _____

6. I can solve word problems
   by guessing and checking.                    Rating: _____

7. I can solve word problems
   by working backwards.                        Rating: _____

8. I can solve word problems
   through logical reasoning
   and trial and error.                         Rating: _____

*Standards-Based MATH Graphic Organizers, Rubrics,*
*and Writing Prompts for Middle Grade Students*

# Assessment Rubric for Rounding Off and Estimation

**Rating Scale:**     **Starting Line**          **Middle of Race**          **Finish Line**

---

1. **Student is able to define and explain the concept of *rounding off*.**
   Starting Line              Middle of Race              Finish Line

2. **Student is able to round numbers off to any factor of ten.**
   Starting Line              Middle of Race              Finish Line

3. **Student is able to define and explain the concept of *estimation*.**
   Starting Line              Middle of Race              Finish Line

4. **Student is able to make reasonable estimations when given sets of numbers to compute.**
   Starting Line              Middle of Race              Finish Line

5. **Student demonstrates understanding of the relationship between rounding off and estimation.**
   Starting Line              Middle of Race              Finish Line

---

Examples of estimation and rounding off problems that I can do:

_____

_____

_____

_____

_____

_____

_____

_____

_____

# Assessment Rubric for Student-led Conference

STUDENT _____ DATE _____

---

**1. You will find the following items in my math portfolio:**

---

**2. While you look at my work, I want you to notice these things about it:**

---

**3. These are the math concepts and skills that I think I know and do well:**

---

**4. The product in my portfolio that I am most proud of is . . .**
   **because . . .**

---

**5. The product in my portfolio that I had the most difficulty with was . . .**
   **because . . .**

---

**6. My math goals for our next conference are:**

---

**7. A final comment I want to make is:**

---

# Assessment for Teamwork or Peer Tutoring on Group Math Projects

**Rating Scale:**     **Very True**          **True**          **Somewhat True**          **Not True**

### 1. We set achievable goals.
Very True          True          Somewhat True          Not True

### 2. We defined group roles.
Very True          True          Somewhat True          Not True

### 3. We accepted individual responsibility.
Very True          True          Somewhat True          Not True

### 4. We helped and encouraged one another to problem solve.
Very True          True          Somewhat True          Not True

### 5. We maintained order in planning and during work sessions.
Very True          True          Somewhat True          Not True

### 6. We stayed on task.
Very True          True          Somewhat True          Not True

### 7. We worked quietly together.
Very True          True          Somewhat True          Not True

### 8. We requested teacher help only when needed.
Very True          True          Somewhat True          Not True

### 9. We listened to one another with respect.
Very True          True          Somewhat True          Not True

### 10. We had success in meeting our established goals.
Very True          True          Somewhat True          Not True

SUMMARY STATEMENT: On the whole I think we:

_____

_____

Signed _____ Date _____

Signed _____ Date _____

# How Do I Really Feel About Math?

**DIRECTIONS:**

On a scale of 1 to 5, with 1 being *Always* and 5 being *Never*, how would you rate each of these statements as they relate to you and your feelings about mathematics?

| | |
|---|---|
| 1. I look forward to math class most of the time. | Rating: _____ |
| 2. I envy students who love math and do it well. | Rating: _____ |
| 3. I enjoy talking to other students about math. | Rating: _____ |
| 4. I willingly take part in math discussions. | Rating: _____ |
| 5. I like to "go to the board" to explain a math concept to the class. | Rating: _____ |
| 6. I settle down to work in math class as soon as the bell rings or the teacher gives directions. | Rating: _____ |
| 7. I can do my math homework without much trouble or help from others. | Rating: _____ |
| 8. I do well on math quizzes and tests. | Rating: _____ |
| 9. When I find something hard to do in math, I stick with it until I get it. | Rating: _____ |
| 10. Math makes me think and apply myself. | Rating: _____ |
| 11. Math is easy for me. | Rating: _____ |
| 12. My math teacher helps me when I need it. | Rating: _____ |

Some other feelings about math I have are:

_____

_____

_____

_____

_____

*Standards-Based MATH Graphic Organizers, Rubrics, and Writing Prompts for Middle Grade Students*

# The Number Report Assessment Rubric

**Rating Scale:**

### 1. Quality of Report Format

My Number Report includes at least ten ample paragraphs
summarizing information I learned through researching my topic;
it also contains a fact file of note cards.                    **Rating:** _____

### 2. Quality of Information

The numerical breakdown of information in my Number Report
makes logical sense and is organized well to cover my topic.   **Rating:** _____

### 3. Grammar

My Number Report contains no grammar or spelling errors.       **Rating:** _____

### 4. Interest

My report uses the number format to make my topic
easier to understand and interesting to read.                 **Rating:** _____

### 5. Graphics/Creativity

My Number Report uses the number format creatively
and my graphics are carefully chosen to enhance the format.   **Rating:** _____

Comments by Student: _____

_____

Overall Rating: _____ Signed _____ Date _____

Comments by Teacher: _____

_____

Overall Rating: _____ Signed _____ Date _____

# Portfolio Assessment Rubric

| Rating Scale: | 1<br>I could have<br>done better | 2<br>I did a<br>good job | 3<br>I did a<br>terrific job |
|---|---|---|---|

## Artifacts

| | | |
|---|---|---|
| 1. Organization and completeness of portfolio | ☐ 1 ☐ 2 ☐ 3 | |
| 2. Quality of artifacts selected | ☐ 1 ☐ 2 ☐ 3 | |
| 3. Creativity shown in work | ☐ 1 ☐ 2 ☐ 3 | |
| 4. Correctness of work (grammar, spelling, sentence structure, neatness, punctuation, etc.) | ☐ 1 ☐ 2 ☐ 3 | |
| 5. Evidence of learning concepts and/or applying skills | ☐ 1 ☐ 2 ☐ 3 | |
| 6. Reflection process | ☐ 1 ☐ 2 ☐ 3 | |
| 7. Evidence of enthusiasm and interest in assignments | ☐ 1 ☐ 2 ☐ 3 | |
| 8. Oral presentation of portfolio | ☐ 1 ☐ 2 ☐ 3 | |

_____

_____

_____

_____

_____

*Standards-Based MATH Graphic Organizers, Rubrics,
and Writing Prompts for Middle Grade Students*

# SELF-ASSESSMENT OR REFLECTIVE QUESTIONS TO CONSIDER WHEN STUDYING A Math TOPIC

Math Concept, Skill or Topic of Study: _____

1. Why is this important?

   _____

2. How does this fit in with what I already know?

   _____

3. What have I learned that is similar to this?

   _____

4. What is the most difficult part of this for me to learn or understand?

   _____

5. How can I use this information in the future?

   _____

6. What have I done to help me understand or learn about this?

   _____

7. What are some questions that I have about this material?

   _____

8. What are some things that I must remember about this material?

   _____

9. What part of this could I teach to someone else?

   _____

10. What part of this do I need more help with in order to process it better?

   _____

Other questions to consider:

_____

_____

_____

# Cooperative Learning Group Performance

**Topic:** _____

**Group Members:** _____

_____

_____

_____

**Date:** _____ **Reporter:** _____

**Rating Scale:**   3 = Outstanding   2 = Satisfactory   1 = Needs Improvement

**Rating:**

| | |
|---|---|
| 1. Each member of the group contributed ideas and suggestions for setting goals, assigning roles, and developing and carrying out a plan of action. | |
| 2. Each member of our group carried out the duties of his or her role. | |
| 3. Each member of our group exhibited respect for the other members. | |
| 4. Each member of our group exhibited good listening skills and an interest in other group members' contributions. | |
| 5. Each member of the group applied conflict resolution skills as appropriate. | |
| 6. Each member of the group contributed to the content focus and overall performance. | |
| 7. A positive, pleasant, and cheerful atmosphere was maintained during group meetings. | |
| 8. Group goals were achieved. | |
| 9. The overall rating we would give our group is . . . | |

*Standards-Based MATH Graphic Organizers, Rubrics, and Writing Prompts for Middle Grade Students*

# Assessment Rubric for Using Bloom's Taxonomy to Evaluate a Product, Performance, or Portfolio

**Type of Product:** _____

**Topic:** _____

---

**Knowledge:** Evidence of learned facts, methods, procedures, or concepts.

| Great Evidence | Ample Evidence | Little Evidence |
|---|---|---|

**Comprehension:** Evidence of understanding of facts, methods, procedures, or concepts.

| Great Evidence | Ample Evidence | Little Evidence |
|---|---|---|

**Application:** Evidence of use of the information in new situations.

| Great Evidence | Ample Evidence | Little Evidence |
|---|---|---|

**Analysis:** Evidence of analysis, recognition of assumptions, and evaluation of relevancy of information.

| Great Evidence | Ample Evidence | Little Evidence |
|---|---|---|

**Synthesis:** Evidence of putting information together in a new and creative way.

| Great Evidence | Ample Evidence | Little Evidence |
|---|---|---|

**Evaluation:** Evidence of acceptance or rejection of information on the basis of criteria.

| Great Evidence | Ample Evidence | Little Evidence |
|---|---|---|

---

Comments by Student: _____

_____

_____

Signed _____ Date _____

Comments by Teacher: _____

_____

_____

Signed _____ Date _____

# Student Assessment of Rubrics As A Means of Measuring Student Progress and/or as an Option for More Traditional Assessment Tools

*Directions: Circle one ([are] or [are not]) in statements 1–7 below and statement 9 on page 108:*

1.  I think rubrics [are] or [are not] a good tool for assessment because:

    _____

    _____

2.  I think letter grades such as A B C D F [are] or [are not] a fair way to assess the quality of a math performance based task because:

    _____

    _____

3.  In my opinion, multiple choice tests [are] or [are not] a good assessment tool for math programs because:

    _____

    _____

4.  In my opinion, teacher made tests [are] or [are not] a good assessment tool for math programs because:

    _____

    _____

5.  In my opinion, standardized tests [are] or [are not] a good assessment tool for math programs because:

    _____

    _____

6.  In my opinion, essay type tests [are] or [are not] a good assessment tool for math programs because:

    _____

    _____

7.  In my opinion, true/false tests [are] or [are not] a good assessment tool for math programs because:

    _____

    _____

8.  If given a choice between teacher-made, true/false tests, essay type questions, multiple choice tests, or rubrics as an assessment to determine my math grade, I would choose

    _____ because:

    _____

*Standards-Based MATH Graphic Organizers, Rubrics, and Writing Prompts for Middle Grade Students*

9. I think the teacher comments [are] or [are not] an important part of rubric assessment form because:

_____

_____

10. I think my parents [understand] or [do not understand] (Circle one) the use of rubrics as an assessment tool and view them as [important] or [not important] (Circle one) in gaining a better understanding of my progress in math.

11. I think rubrics help me to communicate [more effectively] or [less effectively] (Circle one) with my teacher and, therefore, to measure my own progress in math [more] or [less] (circle one) than do traditional pencil and paper quizzes or end of chapter test questions.

12. The strengths and weaknesses of rubrics as a quantitative measure of my progress in math as I see them are:

Strengths: _____

_____

_____

Weaknesses: _____

_____

_____

On the whole, I would rate their value as an assessment tool as currently used in our math program as: (Circle One)

Extremely Valuable: Meaning and intent is clear, provides pertinent information for planning further study, and points out strengths and weaknesses of my work

Somewhat Valuable: Provides some insights to my progress and grasp of the knowledge and concepts studied, helps me to evaluate my performance, and plan for future study

Not Very Valuable: Meaning and intent are unclear; feedback is not especially relative and gives me little concrete information about my overall progress or help in planning for improvement of future work

In a summary statement of three sentences or less, I would say rubrics as a math assessment tool are:

_____

_____

_____

_____

_____

_____

*Standards-Based MATH Graphic Organizers, Rubrics, and Writing Prompts for Middle Grade Students*

# Teacher's Math Curriculum Assessment

1. **My curriculum plan for the year is well organized to adhere to national and state standards, and to cover all the skills and content mandated for my grade level.**

   _____          _____          _____          _____
   Absolutely          I think so          I hope so          I don't know

   Notes/Comments: _____

   _____

2. **My curriculum plan allows room for meeting individual student needs.**

   _____          _____          _____          _____
   Absolutely          I think so          I hope so          I don't know

   Notes/Comments: _____

   _____

3. **My plan includes a good balance of directed instruction, large and small group work including cooperative learning and flexible groups, and independent study.**

   _____          _____          _____          _____
   Absolutely          I think so          I hope so          I don't know

   Notes/Comments: _____

   _____

4. **Opportunities for student participation and the employment of active learning strategies are prevalent throughout my plan.**

   _____          _____          _____          _____
   Absolutely          I think so          I hope so          I don't know

   Notes/Comments: _____

   _____

_Standards-Based MATH Graphic Organizers, Rubrics, and Writing Prompts for Middle Grade Students_

5. **I have planned for authentic assessment of student progress, as well as for any required traditional methods of assessment such as standardized tests and letter grades where required by the school system.**

| Absolutely | I think so | I hope so | I don't know |

Notes/Comments: _____

_____

_____

6. **My plan is feasible in terms of time and resources available.**

| Absolutely | I think so | I hope so | I don't know |

Notes/Comments: _____

_____

_____

7. **I have planned blocks of time to allow flexibility for maximizing those "teachable moments" that encourage spontaneously and foster creativity.**

| Absolutely | I think so | I hope so | I don't know |

Notes/Comments: _____

_____

_____

8. **My curriculum goals are realistic and achievable yet ambitious in terms of student achievement.**

| Absolutely | I think so | I hope so | I don't know |

Notes/Comments: _____

_____

_____

**9.** My plan provides enrichment activities and time for reflection appropriate to the age level and subject I teach.

_____     _____     _____     _____
Absolutely      I think so      I hope so      I don't know

Notes/Comments: _____

_____

**10.** My plan includes provision for parent communication.

_____     _____     _____     _____
Absolutely      I think so      I hope so      I don't know

Notes/Comments: _____

_____

**11.** My plan is consistent with school goals, administrative expectancies, and will allow for cooperation and partnership with the larger school community.

_____     _____     _____     _____
Absolutely      I think so      I hope so      I don't know

Notes/Comments: _____

_____

**12.** I have reviewed my plan carefully and feel that it is a truly excellent program.

_____     _____     _____     _____
Absolutely      I think so      I hope so      I don't know

Notes/Comments: _____

_____

**Reflection:**

After considering the soundness of my curriculum plan for the year as reflected by this assessment tool, I feel that I should make the following additions, deletions, or modifications.

_____

_____

_____

Date: _____

# Questions for Teachers and Students to Consider About Using Rubrics in the Classroom

1. What is a rubric and what kinds of rubrics are there?
   _____

2. What are some characteristics of effective rubrics?
   _____

3. What are the critical components in the design of rubrics?
   _____

4. What is a holistic rubric?
   _____

5. What is an analytical rubric?
   _____

6. Are rubrics developed by students, by teachers, or both?
   _____

7. How does one decide on the criteria of a given rubric?
   _____

8. How does one determine the best type of rating scale for a given rubric?
   _____

9. Are rubrics appropriate for all types of instruction and all types of content areas?
   _____

10. How does one teach students to use and value rubrics as an assessment tool?
    _____

11. Why are rubrics an effective way to measure student performance?
    _____

12. Are rubrics appropriate for measuring the quality of a student-generated product?
    _____

13. How does one translate the results of a rubric into a numerical grade?
    _____

14. How does one use rubrics to guide evaluation and establish a shared standard of quality work?
    _____

15. Are the development and use of rubrics more time consuming for students and teachers as an assessment tool and, if so, is that time commitment worth the effort?
    _____

*Standards-Based MATH Graphic Organizers, Rubrics, and Writing Prompts for Middle Grade Students*

Copyright ©2001 by Incentive Publications, Inc.
Nashville, TN.

# Appendix

National Mathematics Standards

Planning Matrix

Understanding and Using Mathematical Symbols

Checklist for Completing Math Homework

Outline for Creating Your Own Rubric

Take Ten Minutes Challenges Calendar

Bloom's Taxonomy

Williams' Taxonomy

Suggestions for Using Graphic Organizers
to Integrate Mathematics into the Total Curriculum

Bibliography

Index

# National Council of Teachers of Mathematics Standards and Definitions

## Math as Problem Solving

In grades 5-8, the mathematics curriculum should include numerous and varied experiences with problem solving as a method of inquiry and application so that students can: Use problem solving approaches to investigate and understand mathematical content, Formulate problems from situations within and outside mathematics, Develop and apply a variety of strategies to solve problems, with emphasis on multi-step and non-routine problems, Verify and interpret results with respect to the original problem situations, Acquire confidence in using mathematics meaningfully.

## Mathematics as Communication

In grades 5-8, the study of mathematics should include opportunities to communicate so that students can: Model situations using oral, written, concrete, pictorial, graphical, and algebraic methods, Reflect on and clarify their own thinking about mathematical ideas, including the role of definitions, Use the skills of reading, listening, and viewing to interpret and evaluate mathematical ideas, Discuss the mathematical ideas and make conjectures and convincing arguments, Appreciate the value of mathematical notation and its role in the development of mathematical ideas.

## Mathematics as Reasoning

In grades 5-8, reasoning shall permeate the mathematics curriculum so that students can: Recognize and apply deductive reasoning processes, with special attention to spatial reasoning and reasoning with proportions and graphs, Make and evaluate mathematical conjectures and arguments, Validate their own thinking, Appreciate the pervasive use and power of reasoning as a part of mathematics.

Reprinted with permission from *Standards for Mathematics for Grades 5–8,* copyright 2001 by the National Council of Teachers of Mathematics.

## Mathematical Connections

In grades 5-8, the mathematics curriculum should include the investigation of mathematical connections so that students can: See mathematics as an integrated whole, Explore problems and describe results using graphical, numerical, physical, algebraic, and verbal mathematical models or representations, Use a mathematical idea to further their understanding of other mathematical ideas, Apply mathematical thinking and modeling to solve problems that arise in other disciplines, such as art, music, psychology, science, and business, Value the role of mathematics in our culture and society.

## Number and Number Relationships

The curriculum should include the investigation of numbers and number relationships so that students can: Understand and use numbers in a variety of equivalent forms in real-world problem situations; Develop number sense for whole numbers, fractions, decimals, integers, and rational numbers; Apply ratios, proportions, and percents in a variety of situations; Investigate relationships among fractions, decimals, and percents in a variety of situations; Represent numerical relationships in 1- and 2-dimensional graphs.

## Number Systems and Number Theory

In grades 5-8, the mathematics curriculum should include the study of number systems and number theory so that students can: Understand and appreciate the need for numbers beyond the whole numbers, Develop and use order relations for whole numbers, fractions, decimals, integers, and rational numbers, Extend their understanding of whole number operations to fractions, decimals, integers, and rational numbers, Understand how the basic arithmetic operations are related to one another, Develop and apply number theory concepts (e.g., primes, factors, and multiples) in real-world and mathematical problem situations.

Reprinted with permission from *Standards for Mathematics for Grades 5–8*, copyright 2001 by the National Council of Teachers of Mathematics.

*Standards-Based MATH Graphic Organizers, Rubrics,*
*and Writing Prompts for Middle Grade Students*

## Computation and Estimation

In grades 5-8, the mathematics curriculum should develop the concepts underlying computation and estimation in various contexts so that students can: Compute with whole numbers, fractions, decimals, integers, and rational numbers, Develop, analyze, and explain procedures for computation and techniques for estimation, Develop, analyze, and explain methods for solving proportions, Select and use an appropriate method for computing from among mental arithmetic, paper-and-pencil, calculator, and computer methods, Use computation, estimation, and proportions to solve problems, and Use estimation to check the reasonableness of results.

## Patterns and Functions

In grades 5-8, the mathematics curriculum should include explorations of patterns and functions so that students can: Describe, extend, analyze, and create a wide variety of patterns, Describe and represent relationships with tables, graphs, and rules, Analyze functional relationships to explain how a change in one quantity results in change in another, Use patterns and functions to represent and solve problems.

## Algebra

In grades 5-8, the mathematics curriculum should include explorations of algebraic concepts and processes so that students can: Understand the concepts of variable, expression, and equation, Represent situations and number patterns with tables, graphs, verbal rules, and equations and explore the interrelationships of these representations, Analyze tables and graphs to identify properties and relationships, Develop confidence in solving linear equations using concrete, informal, and formal methods, Investigate inequalities and nonlinear equations informally, Apply algebraic methods to solve a variety of real-world and mathematical problems.

Reprinted with permission from *Standards for Mathematics for Grades 5–8*, copyright 2001 by the National Council of Teachers of Mathematics.

## Statistics

In grades 5-8, the mathematics curriculum should include exploration of statistics in real-world situations so that students can: Systematically collect, organize, and describe date, Construct, read, and interpret tables, charts, and graphs, Make inferences and convincing arguments that are based on data analysis, Evaluate arguments that are based on data analysis, and Develop an appreciation for statistical methods as powerful means for decision-making.

## Probability

In grades 5-8, the mathematics curriculum should include explorations of probability in real-world situations so that students can: Model situations by devising and carrying out experiments or simulations to determine probabilities, Model situations by constructing a sample space to determine probabilities, Appreciate the power of using a probability model by comparing experimental results with mathematical expectations, Make predictions that are based on experimental or theoretical probabilities, Develop an appreciation for the pervasive use of probability in the real world.

## Geometry

In grades 5-8, the mathematics curriculum should include the study of the geometry of one, two, and three dimensions in a variety of situations so that students can: Identify, describe, compare, and classify geometric figures, Visualize and represent geometric figures with special attention to developing spatial sense, Explore transformations of geometric figures, Represent and solve problems using geometric models, Understand and apply geometric properties and relationships, and Develop an appreciation of geometry as a means of describing the physical world.

## Measurement

In grades 5-8, the mathematics curriculum should include extensive concrete experiences using measurement so that students can: Extend their understanding of the process of measurement, Estimate, make, and use measurements to describe and compare phenomena, Select appropriate units and tools to measure to the degree of accuracy required in a particular situation, Understand the structure and use of systems of measurement, Extend their understanding of the concepts of perimeter, area, volume, angle measure, capacity, and weight and mass, Develop the concepts of rate and other derived and indirect measurements, and Develop formulas and procedures for determining measures to solve problems.

**Reprinted with permission from *Standards for Mathematics for Grades 5–8*, copyright 2001 by the National Council of Teachers of Mathematics.**

*Standards-Based MATH Graphic Organizers, Rubrics,*
*and Writing Prompts for Middle Grade Students*

# Planning Matrix

**Correlatives: National Mathematics Standards as identified by the National Council of Teachers of Mathematics with activities and projects in Standards-Based Graphic Organizers, Rubrics, and Writing Prompts, Incentive Publications, 2001.**

| Standards | Graphic Organizers | Writing Prompts | Rubrics | Reinforcement & Reflection |
|---|---|---|---|---|
| **Mathematics as Problem Solving** | 12, 16, 17, 20, 26, 27, 34, 37, 43 | 56, 63, 64, 75 | 93, 96, 97, 102, 103 | 10, 50, 52, 102, 103, 114 |
| **Mathematics as Communication** | 11, 17, 18, 21, 24, 36, 39, 45 | 53, 55, 56, 61, 63, 66, 68, 73, 74, 76, 132 | 88, 89, 95, 100, 102, 103, 104, 130, 131 | 10, 50, 52, 100, 102, 103, 104, 114, 122, 123, 126, 127, 130, 131, 132 |
| **Mathematics as Reasoning** | 13, 19, 20, 29, 40, 41, 42 | 54, 60, 65, 67 | 93, 96, 97, 102, 103, 107, 108 | 10, 50, 52, 102, 103, 107, 108, 114, 127 |
| **Mathematical Connections** | 11, 13, 15, 18, 23, 25, 28, 33, 38, 49 | 53, 54, 57, 61, 62, 75 | 89, 92, 94, 102, 103 | 10, 23, 49, 50, 52, 99, 102, 103, 115, 126, 139, 140 |

# Planning Matrix

**Correlatives: National Mathematics Standards as identified by the National Council of Teachers of Mathematics with activities and projects in Standards-Based Graphic Organizers, Rubrics, and Writing Prompts, Incentive Publications, 2001.**

| Standards | Graphic Organizers | Writing Prompts | Rubrics | Reinforcement & Reflection |
|---|---|---|---|---|
| **Number and Number Relationships** | 15, 16, 23, 32, 33, 35, 48 | 57, 58, 61, 62, 66 | 78, 90, 102, 103, 106, 112 | 102, 103, 112, 115, 126, 133 |
| **Number Systems and Number Theory** | 11, 15, 23, 25, 32, 48 | 58, 59, 67, 70 | 90, 101, 102, 103, 105, 106, 109, 110 | 102, 103, 106, 109, 110, 115, 124, 126, 133 |
| **Computation and Estimation** | 14, 22, 31, 47 | 70, 71, 72 | 79, 87, 91, 92, 98 | 116, 125, 126, 128, 129 |

*Standards-Based MATH Graphic Organizers, Rubrics, and Writing Prompts for Middle Grade Students*

# Planning Matrix

**Correlatives: National Mathematics Standards as identified by the National Council of Teachers of Mathematics with activities and projects in Standards-Based Graphic Organizers, Rubrics, and Writing Prompts, Incentive Publications, 2001.**

| Standards | Graphic Organizers | Writing Prompts | Rubrics | Reinforcement & Reflection |
|---|---|---|---|---|
| **Patterns and Functions** | 14, 16, 21, 30, 35, 44 | 53, 59, 72 | 89, 90, 92, 93, 95 | 116, 125, 126, 128, 129 |
| **Algebra** | 16, 20, 23, 35, 42, 43, 48 | 60, 61, 62, 66 | 92, 93, 95 | 116, 125, 126, 128, 129 |
| **Statistics** | 22, 23, 46, 47, 48 | 64, 65, 70 | 89, 90, 92, 93, 95 | 117, 125, 126, 128, 129 |

*Standards-Based MATH Graphic Organizers, Rubrics, and Writing Prompts for Middle Grade Students*

Copyright ©2001 by Incentive Publications, Inc. Nashville, TN.

# Planning Matrix

**Correlatives: National Mathematics Standards as identified by the National Council of Teachers of Mathematics with activities and projects in Standards-Based Graphic Organizers, Rubrics, and Writing Prompts, Incentive Publications, 2001.**

| Standards | Graphic Organizers | Writing Prompts | Rubrics | Reinforcement & Reflection |
|---|---|---|---|---|
| Probability | 12, 13, 14, 15, 26, 29, 30, 32 | 62, 64, 69, 70 | 90, 92, 93, 95 | 117, 125, 126, 128, 129 |
| Geometry | 11, 14, 16, 22, 24, 31, 34, 47 | 55, 63, 67, 68, 73 | 80, 81, 86, 92, 93, 95 | 117, 125, 126, 128, 129 |
| Measurement | 11, 13, 22, 24, 29, 47 | 56, 68, 69 | 82, 83, 84, 85, 92, 93, 95 | 117, 125, 126, 128, 129 |

# Math Words
## to Know and Use

| | | |
|---|---|---|
| Abacus | Cone | Fahrenheit scale |
| Absolute value | Congruent | Flip |
| Acute angle | Cube | Fraction |
| Addend | Cycloid | Frequency |
| Addition | Data | Function |
| Adjacent angle | Decagon | Geometric |
| Algorithm | Decimal | Geometry |
| Angle | Degree | Gram |
| Arc | Denominator | Graph |
| Associative property | Diagonal | Grid |
| Average | Diameter | Hemisphere |
| Axis | Difference | Heptagon |
| Base | Digit | Hexagon |
| Bisect | Distributive property | Horizontal |
| Calculator | Dividend | Hypotenuse |
| Cardinal number | Divisible | Icosahedrons |
| Centigrade scale | Division | Improper fraction |
| Centimeter | Dodecahedron | Integer |
| Central angle | Edge | Intersecting line |
| Chord | Elements | Inverse |
| Circle | Empty set | Kilogram |
| Circumference | Endpoint | Latitude |
| Common denominator | Equation | Least common denominator |
| Common factor | Equilateral | Least common multiple |
| Common multiple | Equivalent | Line |
| Common number | Estimate | Line segment |
| Compass | Even number | Longitude |
| Complementary angle | Face | Manipulative |
| Composite number | Factor | Mathematician |

Standards-Based MATH Graphic Organizers, Rubrics, and Writing Prompts for Middle Grade Students

| | | |
|---|---|---|
| Mean | Perpendicular line | Set |
| Measurement | Pi | Similarity |
| Median | Pictograph | Skip count |
| Meter | Place value | Slide rule |
| Metric | Plane | Solution |
| Midpoint | Point | Spectrum |
| Millimeter | Polygon | Sphere |
| Mixed numeral | Polyhedron | Square |
| Mode | Prime number | Square root |
| Multiple | Prism | Statistics |
| Multiplication | Probability | Straight angle |
| Multiplier | Product | Sum |
| Negative integer | Proper fraction | Supplementary angle |
| Nonagon | Proportion | Symmetry |
| Number line | Protractor | Tangent |
| Number systems | Pythagorean theorem | Tessellations |
| Numeral | Quadrilateral | Theorems |
| Numerator | Quotient | Trapezoid |
| Obtuse angle | Radius | Triangle |
| Octagon | Random | Turn |
| Octahedron | Ratio | Variable |
| Odd number | Rational numbers | Venire |
| Opposite property | Ray | Venn diagram |
| Ordered pair | Reciprocals | Vertex |
| Ordinal number | Rectangle | Vertical |
| Palindrome | Reflex angle | Volume |
| Parallel line | Remainder | Whole number |
| Parallelogram | Rhombus | X-Axis |
| Pentagon | Right angle | Y-Axis |
| Percentage | Rounding | Yardstick |
| Perimeter | Segment | Zero |

# Word-a-Day Calendar Outline

Use words from the **MATH WORDS TO KNOW AND USE** page and from your textbook to create your own word-a-day calendar. Make a new list for every month and keep it in your notebook for ready reference.

| 1 | 2 | 3 | 4 | 5 |
|---|---|---|---|---|
| 6 | 7 | 8 | 9 | 10 |
| 11 | 12 | 13 | 14 | 15 |
| 16 | 17 | 18 | 19 | 20 |

*Standards-Based MATH Graphic Organizers, Rubrics, and Writing Prompts for Middle Grade Students*

# Understanding and Using Mathematical Symbols

## MATHEMATICAL SYMBOLS

| | | | |
|---|---|---|---|
| $ | dollars | ≠ | is not equal to |
| ¢ | cents | < | is less than |
| ø | empty set | > | is greater than |
| {} | empty set | ≥ | is greater than or equal to |
| % | percent | ≤ | is less than or equal to |
| π | pi (3.14159) | ≈ | is approximately equal to |
| ° | degrees | ~ | is similar to |
| F | Fahrenheit | ≅ | is congruent to |
| C | centigrade | ≇ | is not congruent to |
| . | point | +4 | positive integer |
| √ | square root | −4 | negative integer |
| ⌢ | arc | ↔ | line |
| ÷ | divide | ⟼ | line segment |
| / | divide | → | ray |
| + | add | ∠ | angle |
| − | subtract | m∠ | measure of angle |
| x | multiply | Δ | triangle |
| • | multiply | ⊥ | perpendicular |
| ∪ | union of sets | ‖ | parallel |
| ∩ | intersection of sets | $a^n$ | a to the $n^{th}$ power |
| = | is equal to | | |

Use the symbols above as reference. Activities on the following page will serve as icebreakers, brain teasers, homework, or peer tutoring assignments, or as creative journal entry sparkers. They could also be used as the first of a series of "read and relate" activities for a classroom collection to be used over and over in a variety of ways to reinforce mathematical facts and concepts.

# Understanding and Using Mathematical Symbols

## Read and Relate Activities

**READ** The mathematical symbol for equality is =. This indicates that the number(s) on both sides of the symbol are equal. When both sides of an equation are not equal, the ≠ (does not equal) sign is used.

**RELATE** Draw 10 symbols which relate to transportation. Use them as symbols in a rebus story about transportation.

---

**READ** Symbols which indicate inequalities are as follows: < (is less than) and > (is greater than). The symbol shows the relationship between the two sides of an equation.

**RELATE** Write a comprehensive response to this question: How do you know if something is half full or half empty?

---

**READ** In the field of geometry, symbols are used to show the relationship of figures. The term "is congruent to" is used instead of the term "equals." The symbol showing congruence is ≈; the symbol for incongruence is ≠.

**RELATE** Design an imaginary figure using a rectangle and the symbols for *equality, less* and *greater than,* and *incongruence.* Name it and tell what it does, where it lives, and how it contributes to society.

---

**READ** Mathematical symbols showing arithmetic operations are + (addition), − (subtraction), x (multiplication), and ÷ (division).

**RELATE** With a friend, compose an eight- to ten-line jingle about how important it is to know the four basic math operations.

---

**READ** A set is a collection of elements. Ancient people understood the concept of sets. In the 19th century, George Boole created symbols for sets. Set symbols include ( ∈ ) element, ( ∍ ) not an element, ( ∪ ) union, ( ∩ ) intersection, and ( ⊂ ) subset.

**RELATE** Write an explanation of why certain groups of people in your school are sometimes thought of as sets. Write about the union and the intersection of these groups.

---

**READ** Symbols are used in the study of geometry to indicate ( ∠ ) angle, (⟷) line, ( O ) circle, (⟶) line segment, ( → ) ray, ( ⊥ ) perpendicular to, ( ‖ ) parallel to, and ( Δ ) triangle.

**RELATE** Use mathematical symbols to create a code of your own. Write a note to a friend using your new code.

---

**READ** In the study of fractions, we deal with factors and multiples. Abbreviations associated with fractions include: LCM, least common multiple; GCF, greatest common factor; GCD, greatest common divisor.

**RELATE** Associate these sets of letters with something else that is important to you. This will help you remember how these letters relate to fractions.

---

**READ** One of two equal factors of a number is called its square root. (5 is the square root of 25 because 5 x 5 = 25). The symbol for square root is $\sqrt{\phantom{x}}$.

**RELATE** Explain the following: square deal, square off, he's a square, square dance, square away, and square shooter.

*Standards-Based MATH Graphic Organizers, Rubrics, and Writing Prompts for Middle Grade Students*

Copyright ©2001 by Incentive Publications, Inc. Nashville, TN.

# Writing In the Area Of Mathematics

**TOTAL SCORE:**

**Comments**                                      Yes        No

1. Did writer compose introductory paragraph?

2. Did writer make clear his/her purpose for writing?

3. Did writer limit one aspect of topic to each paragraph?

4. Did the writer use supporting details to clarify topic in each paragraph?

5. Did writer organize his paragraphs in a logical sequence?

6. Did writer use clear transitions between paragraphs?

7. Did writer bring topic to a sufficient close in concluding paragraph?

8. Did writer choose appropriate title for topic?

9. Did writer use correct grammar, usage, spelling, capitalization and punctuation in paragraphs?

10. Did writer proofread the final copy?

# Completing Math Homework

DIRECTIONS: After each statement below, indicate the student's overall level of performance in completing homework assignments for a given time period.

| Homework Habit | A<br>Always | S<br>Sometimes | R<br>Rarely |
|---|:---:|:---:|:---:|
| 1. Student understands importance of completing homework tasks. | A | S | R |
| 2. Student writes down homework tasks when given. | A | S | R |
| 3. Student knows what resources are needed to complete homework tasks. | A | S | R |
| 4. Student takes appropriate resources home to complete assigned tasks. | A | S | R |
| 5. Student has adequate place and time at home to complete assigned tasks. | A | S | R |
| 6. Student completes homework tasks on regular basis. | A | S | R |
| 7. Student remembers to bring homework tasks back to school on time. | A | S | R |
| 8. Student does well on homework tasks. | A | S | R |
| 9. Student learns from homework tasks. | A | S | R |
| 10. Student corrects mistakes on homework tasks. | A | S | R |

Comments from Student: _____

_____

_____

_____

Comments from Teacher: _____

_____

_____

_____

# Math Test Taking

Plus (+)   Minus (–)

## PREPARATIONS FOR THE TEST

___    ___    1. Student knows date and time for test.

___    ___    2. Student has adequate review notes for test.

___    ___    3. Student has study buddy or study group to work with in preparing for test.

___    ___    4. Student appears to understand concepts to be included on test.

___    ___    5. Student feels comfortable asking questions of teacher or peers about the test.

___    ___    6. Student comes to class prepared to take the test.

## DURING THE TEST

___    ___    1. Student reads through questions on test before starting.

___    ___    2. Student appears to understand directions and time constraints for taking the test.

___    ___    3. Student moves through test answering questions he/she knows first and leaves those he/she is unsure of for later.

___    ___    4. Student double-checks answers to questions/problems before moving on to other questions or before turning test in to teacher.

___    ___    5. Student knows when it is appropriate to guess at answers and when to leave answers blank.

## FOLLOWING THE TEST

___    ___    1. Student perceives test as fair.

___    ___    2. Student understands and accepts grade on test.

___    ___    3. Student knows what he/she did incorrectly on test.

*Standards-Based MATH Graphic Organizers, Rubrics,*
*and Writing Prompts for Middle Grade Students*

# Criteria for Creating Your Own Rubric

## Excellent

My portfolio, project, or task
1. is complete.
2. is well-organized.
3. is visually exciting.
4. shows much evidence of multiple resources.
5. shows much evidence of problem solving, decision making, and higher-order thinking skills.
6. reflects enthusiasm for the subject.
7. contains additional work beyond the requirements.
8. communicates effectively what I have learned in keeping with my learning objectives.
9. includes highly efficient assessment tools and makes ample provisions for meta-cognitive reflection.
10. has identified many future learning goals in keeping with my own needs and interests.

## Good

My portfolio, project, or task
1. is complete.
2. is well-organized.
3. is interesting.
4. shows some evidence of multiple resources.
5. shows some evidence of problem solving, decision making, and higher-order thinking skills.
6. reflects some interest for the topic.
7. contains a small amount of work beyond the requirements.
8. communicates some things I have learned in keeping with my learning objectives.
9. includes effective assessment tools and reflective comments.
10. has identified some future learning goals in keeping with my own needs and interests.

## Needs Improvement

My portfolio, project, or task
1. is incomplete.
2. is poorly organized.
3. is not very interesting to others.
4. shows little or almost no evidence of multiple resources.
5. shows little or almost no evidence of problem solving, decision making, and higher-order thinking skills.
6. reflects little interest in the subject.
7. contains no additional work beyond the minimum requirements.
8. communicates few things that I have truly learned in keeping with my objectives.
9. includes few examples of self assessment tools and reflective comments.
10. has identified no future learning goals in keeping with my own needs and interests.

Standards-Based MATH Graphic Organizers, Rubrics, and Writing Prompts for Middle Grade Students

# Outline for Creating Your Own Rubric

Use this outline and the criteria for creating your own rubric to create a holistic or analytic rubric for evaluating a portfolio, project, or task. A holistic rubric assigns levels of performance with descriptors for each level. An analytic rubric assigns levels of performance with numerical points allocated for every descriptor at each level.

## Excellent Levels

Descriptors:                                                          Points Awarded:

_____                    _____

_____                    _____

_____                    _____

## Good Levels

Descriptors:                                                          Points Awarded:

_____                    _____

_____                    _____

_____                    _____

## Needs Improvement

Descriptors:                                                          Points Awarded:

_____                    _____

_____                    _____

_____                    _____

NOTE: You can add additional levels and descriptors as needed. You can also create your own labels for the levels and use such categories as: Exemplary Achievement, Commendable Achievement, Limited Evidence of Achievement, and Minimal Achievement or simply top levels, medium levels, or needs improvement levels.

Comments by Student: _____

_____

Signed _____ Date _____

Comments by Teacher: _____

_____

Signed _____ Date _____

# A Calendar of Creative Thinking and Writing Sparkers to Encourage the Use of Math Skills and Concepts Across the Curriculum

**1** Define the word *abacus* and give some information about its history. Write a dialogue between an abacus and a computer where each is justifying its importance.

**2** Invent a new geometric shape and write its definition and instructions for use.

**3** Write a poem, story, or song about some way or an instance in which geometry is reflected in nature.

**4** Write a humorous story with the title "Before the Days of Computers."

**5** Make a measurement drawing according to the following directions: Draw a skyscraper $8\frac{1}{2}$ inches high with a roof span $5\frac{3}{4}$ inches across. Draw a crow ($1\frac{1}{4}$ inch) on the rooftop. Draw a tree $4\frac{3}{4}$ inches tall with a trunk $2\frac{1}{4}$ inches wide. Draw a truck $3\frac{1}{2}$ inches long and $1\frac{4}{5}$ inches wide, and at least 2 inches distance from the tree.

**6** Make a list of mathematical formulas and computations that are used in carrying out science experiments.

**7** Construct a flowchart to show how the school board is selected in your community.

**8** Plan a survey of your classmates to determine the most popular sports, musical, or political hero of the day. Select a graphic organizer to use to report your findings.

**9** Write a paragraph critiquing the math textbook used for your grade. Be as specific as you can about weaknesses and strengths.

**10** Make a list of ten story starters that could be used to create math journal entries that your classmates would want to write.

**11** Select a famous mathematician from the past and one from the present to compare and contrast the importance of their work and its lasting contribution to mankind.

**12** Use geometric shapes to create a design for a book cover for an art book by a photographer famous for his environmental shots devoted to saving endangered plant species.

**13** Create a learning poster devoted to fractions.

**14** Develop a timeline to show the important steps in the development and use of the computer as an instructional tool.

**15** Relate to and write a paragraph explaining your reaction to the statement, "some students are better at math than others."

**16** Plan your dream trip. Use a map and compute the total number of miles you will travel.

**17** Write a creative story or a comic strip about "The poor little square who wanted to be a circle, until she met a triangle."

**18** Use one of the following as the theme of a cartoon, rap or jingle: "Don't Tangle with an Angle," "Nobody Should Wrestle with a Decimal," "Do You Really Believe Money Grows on Trees?" "You Can't Argue with Fraction Action."

**19** Design a machine that would automatically complete math homework assignments, take math tests, and even scan and underline important facts in math textbooks. How much would it be worth to you?

**20** Make up a budget for yourself for the next 30 days. Include all expected expenses. Then, just for fun, pretend you have an extra $100 to spend. Include this windfall in your budget.

*Standards-Based MATH Graphic Organizers, Rubrics, and Writing Prompts for Middle Grade Students*

Copyright ©2001 by Incentive Publications, Inc. Nashville, TN.

# Take Ten Minutes Challenges Calendar

| 1 | 2 | 3 | 4 | 5 |
|---|---|---|---|---|
| Write ten sensible sentences using the word **equation**. | Make a list of (ten times ten, plus ten) even numbers. | Write the names and make sketches of ten different shapes. | Write ten (ten minus three) - digit numbers. | Write the numbers ten billion, ten million, ten thousand, and ten. Find the sum of the numbers. |
| **6** | **7** | **8** | **9** | **10** |
| Use ten different-sized triangles to design a tree, a tepee, or a tower. | Write ten math word problems. | Exchange your ten math word problems with a classmate. You solve his or hers; he or she solves yours. | Write ten good hints for preparing for and taking a math test. | Thumb through your math textbook to find ten assignments or activities that look especially difficult to you. Mark these places and discuss the activities with a friend. |
| **11** | **12** | **13** | **14** | **15** |
| List ten topics that you might consider for a math fair project. Rate them 1 to 10 (1 is lowest, 10 is highest) according to their interest to you. | Make a list of ten things you would buy if someone gave you a million dollars with the provision that it be spent in ten days for ten individual items whose prices total exactly one million dollars. Assign a specific value to each item. | Devise ten good test items for a math quiz for your class. | Compose a ten-verse rap, chant, or jingle using ten words only for each verse. | Write ten math riddles— complete with answers, of course. |
| **16** | **17** | **18** | **19** | **20** |
| Compare and contrast algebra and geometry. Use a Venn diagram to show ten differences and/or ten likenesses. | List ten math terms that are important for students of your age to know. Write brief definitions of each of the ten terms. | Draw and label ten different math tools that are used in your school. | In the center of your paper, sketch an average-sized orange. On the right-hand side of the paper, sketch ten round things that are smaller than an orange. On the left-hand side, sketch ten round things that are larger. | Use ten numbers that are important to you personally (address, phone number, age, etc.) to create a "me" poster. |

From *Integrating Instruction in Math: Strategies, Activities, Projects, Tools, and Techniques* by Imogene Forte and Sandra Schurr; Copyright 1996, Incentive Publications, Inc. Nashville, TN.

*Standards-Based MATH Graphic Organizers, Rubrics, and Writing Prompts for Middle Grade Students*

# BLOOM'S CHART

Bloom's Taxonomy, developed by Benjamin Bloom, provides a hierarchy of critical thinking skills arranged in an increasing order of difficulty. Knowing about the different levels of thinking can help you perform well on papers, tests, and homework. Often scores will increase if you include something in your answer, paper, or project that shows you have analyzed, synthesized, or evaluated the subject matter. Studying the definitions and verbs below will help you apply these thinking levels to your own study habits. The sample tasks will help you think of projects that show your greater understanding of the subject matter.

Knowing about the different levels of thinking can help you perform well on papers, tests, and homework. Often scores will increase if you include something in your answer, paper, or project that shows you have **analyzed, synthesized,** or **evaluated** the subject matter. Studying the definitions and verbs below will help you apply these thinking levels to your own study habits. The sample tasks will help you think of projects that show your greater understanding of the subject matter.

| LEVELS | VERBS | SAMPLE TASKS |
|---|---|---|
| **KNOWLEDGE** *Learn terms, facts, methods, procedures, concepts* | Draw, Count, Group, Memorize, Point, Follow directions, Recognize, Reproduce, State, Tabulate | 1. Recognize the many places we still find Roman numerals in use today, such as on clock and watch faces, on monuments and building inscriptions, and on official papers, magazines, and books. 2. Point out examples of symmetry in nature. |
| **COMPREHENSION** *Understand uses and implications of terms, facts, methods, procedures, concepts* | Change, Classify, Convert, Estimate, Interpret, Express in other terms, Measure, Put in order, Show, Suggest | 1. Round off and estimate the answers to a variety of whole number problems. Work the problems to determine the accuracy of your estimated answers. 2. Express in monetary terms what you think the following money-related talk really means: *break the bank, dough, greenbacks, moolah, sawbuck,* and *two bits.* |
| **APPLICATION** *Practice theory, solve problems, use information in new situations* | Calculate, Compute, Construct, Derive, Graph, Manipulate, Operate, Practice, Prove, Solve | 1. Compute a set of measurement conversion challenges to show the efficiency of the metric system over the English system. 2. Graph the results of a survey which you have conducted, using at least two of the following types of graphs: line graph, bar graph, pictograph, or circle graph. |
| **ANALYSIS** *Analyze structure, recognize assumptions and poor logic, evaluate relevancy* | Break down, Deduce, Diagram, Distinguish, Formulate, Group, Order, Separate, Simplify, Sort | 1. Break down a group of word problems according to the type of operation(s) required to solve them correctly. 2. Select a mathematical principle, skill, or concept and simplify it in terms that a younger student could understand through illustrations, diagrams, explanation, and examples. |
| **SYNTHESIS** *Write theme, present speech, plan experiment, put information together in a new and creative way* Construct    Predict | Derive, Document, Generate, Integrate, Prepare, Propose, Specify, Tell | 1. Derive how you think different mathematical theories have been used and are applied in the real world today. 2. Integrate mathematics with another subject or course you are taking through the development of a creative report or project that includes skills and concepts from both disciplines. |
| **EVALUATION** *Set standards, judge with purpose, accept or reject on basis of criteria* | Appraise, Choose, Compare, Conclude, Decide, Describe, Evaluate, Justify, Measure, Validate | 1. Contrast the measurement terms used at sea and the measurement terms used on land. 2. Evaluate the mandatory use of the metric system over the English system of measurement in business and industry throughout the United States. |

*Standards-Based MATH Graphic Organizers, Rubrics, and Writing Prompts for Middle Grade Students*

Copyright ©2001 by Incentive Publications, Inc. Nashville, TN.

# Weight

**ANALYSIS:** Compare and contrast the metric and the standard units of measure. Identify the advantages and disadvantages of each.

**COMPREHENSION:** Determine which standard unit <u>and</u> which metric unit you would use to measure each of these:
- your weight
- a letter
- a sack of potatoes
- a loaf of bread
- an elephant
- a baseball

**KNOWLEDGE:** Recall all the standard and metric units of weight you can think of; then check your list against those found in your math textbook. Add those you missed.

**EVALUATION:** Decide which system works best for measuring weight, the standard or the metric. Defend your position.

**SYNTHESIS:** Invent a new system for measuring weight. Give your units names and explain how the system works. Design a poster to advertise this new measurement system to your class.

**APPLICATION:** Predict in what order the following would be arranged, from the heaviest to the lightest. Then weigh each item to see if your prediction was correct.
- paperclip
- dime
- eraser
- pencil
- index card
- comb

*Standards-Based MATH Graphic Organizers, Rubrics, and Writing Prompts for Middle Grade Students*

# Outline Arranged According to Bloom's Taxonomy for Developing a Project or Lesson Plan for a Math Topic

Topic: _____

## KNOWLEDGE

1. List questions that you would like to answer about the topic.

2. Identify and define key words or terms related to the topic.

3. List resources that can be used to locate information related to the topic.

## COMPREHENSION

1. Make a study plan for finding out all you can about the topic.

2. Summarize important facts and/or concepts you need to find.

3. Describe ways that you might share the information you gather.

## APPLICATION

1. Plan an interview with someone very knowledgeable about the topic.

2. Design a model to show something important about the topic.

3. Plan to make an experiment to demonstrate a key idea related to the topic.

## ANALYSIS

1. Compare and contrast some aspect of the topic with that of a related topic.

2. Separate the topic into several subtopics.

3. Plan a survey to demonstrate what your classmates know about the topic.

## SYNTHESIS

1. Create a list of predictions related to the topic.

2. Compose a poem or short story about the topic.

3. Design a series of drawings or diagrams to demonstrate facts and or concepts related to the topic.

## EVALUATION

1. Determine the most important facts and/or concepts you have learned about the topic. Order the facts or concepts from most important to least important, giving reasons for your choices.

2. Criticize a resource you used and give recommendations for improving it.

*Standards-Based MATH Graphic Organizers, Rubrics, and Writing Prompts for Middle Grade Students*

# Williams' Taxonomy

Williams' Taxonomy of Creative Thought was developed by Frank Williams for use in teaching creative thinking skills. It can be especially helpful for developing tasks that are spatial, flexible, spontaneous, analogical and/or divergent. It includes eight levels arranged in a hierarchy with certain behaviors associated with each level. The first four levels are cognitive in nature while the last four levels are affective in nature. The following overview of the taxonomy includes a few selected cue words to be used to trigger responses to a given creative challenge or stimulus.

While Bloom's Taxonomy is used for teaching critical thinking skills, Williams' Taxonomy is used for teaching creative thinking skills. Although there is a relationship between these two models, and even some overlap, it should be noted that critical thinking tends to be more reactive and vertical in nature while creative thinking tends to be more proactive and lateral in nature. Another way of saying this is that critical thinking tends to involve tasks that are logical, rational, sequential, analytical, and convergent. Creative thinking, on the other hand, tends to involve tasks that are spatial, flexible, spontaneous, analogical, and divergent. Critical thinking is "left brain" thinking while creative thinking is "right brain" thinking.

It is strongly suggested that a teacher keep a copy of Williams' Taxonomy in the lesson plan book so that the levels and behaviors can be an integral part of most lesson plans and student assignments. On the opposite page is a brief overview of the levels in Williams' Taxonomy. Each level is accompanied by a few cue words to be used to trigger student responses to a given creative stimulus or challenge.

*Standards-Based MATH Graphic Organizers, Rubrics,*
*and Writing Prompts for Middle Grade Students*

# A High Probability Lesson Plan

**FLUENCY**

Write a paragraph on the topic of using reference materials as a tool for student success. Tell why they are necessary, where they can be located, and the penalties paid for carelessness in their use.

**FLEXIBILITY**

Create a poster illustrating as many types of reference materials as you can think of which are available to students in your school.

**ORIGINALITY**

Some common forms of reference materials found in most school libraries are encyclopedias, world almanacs, dictionaries, thesauruses, magazines, and newspapers. List each of these reference tools on a sheet of paper and try to give at least one way each one could be used in an unusual manner to aid students in your school to develop more original and/or creative content-based reports or projects.

**ELABORATION**

Elaborate on this statement: "You will find it a very good practice always to verify your references, sir."

— Martin Joseph Routh

**RISK TAKING**

Write a position paper, to discuss in a total group setting, on "using reference materials to promote cooperative learning and group interaction as opposed to the traditional independent research paper."

**COMPLEXITY**

Devise a skit to demonstrate ways reference materials have been abused or overused by teachers and students in the traditional test-centered classrooms.

**CURIOSITY**

Select a math, social studies, or science topic that you would like to (or need to) know more about. Develop a lesson plan complete with the time table and list of questions to answer. List the reference materials you will need to complete the study.

**IMAGINATION**

Imagine what the world would be like if there were no written or recorded reference materials, and everyone had to rely on oral communication and imagination.

*Standards-Based MATH Graphic Organizers, Rubrics, and Writing Prompts for Middle Grade Students*

# Suggestions for Using Graphic Organizers to Integrate Mathematics into the Total Curriculum

1. Use concept webs or other advanced organizers to explain mathematical ideas as they relate to historical events or current happenings.
   *Example:* Give a speech on current stock market trends or the construction of the Eiffel Tower.

2. Construct flowcharts or diagrams to show processes for completing a specific task related to gathering and disseminating facts and/or information about a mathematical issue of concern to people of your age.
   *Example:* Use a flowchart to plan and develop a research project on the cost of lunch at your school.

3. Design a puppet show storyboard that shows parts of the development of a mathematical concept. Remember that a storyboard does not attempt to show all of the scenes in a story, but merely serves as an outline for the major people, places, and events.

4. Design a explanatory chart to show an audience the relationships, sequences, or positions that exist within an institution, group, or collection of data. Consider any topic for this chart, from the organization of the various branches of military services, to the types of food chains in natural habitats, to the interactions of fictional characters.

5. Use one or more graphic organizers to prepare a presentation. Some graphic organizers to consider are a Venn diagram, a Production Web, or a Graph Matrix. This type of presentation is designed to appeal to a person's ability to reason or to a person's ability to feel emotions. Arrange your arguments so that they:
   (1) ask a question and then answer it;
   (2) relate an anecdote, observation, or experience; and
   (3) state a fact or statistic.

6. Use a Book Report organizer to plan a report on a biography of a famous person in the history of mathematics. As you prepare the report, think about your reactions to the events in the figure's life that please or bother you, situations that surprise or dazzle you, and obstacles that challenge or disappoint you.

7. Use Venn diagrams to compare and contrast people, places, and mathematical concepts being studied.
   *Example:* Compare and contrast the differing methods of solving a complex word problem.

8. Construct line graphs, pictographs, bar graphs, or circle graphs to organize and present data related to class surveys, research findings, or community poll results.

9. Use time lines to establish the chronology of important events such as the sequence of mathematical events leading up to the successful development of rockets.

10. Identify cause and effect situations and construct a cause and effect chart to show the sequence and impact.
    *Example:* Graphically show the influence of technology in today's schools on the workplace of tomorrow.

*Standards-Based MATH Graphic Organizers, Rubrics, and Writing Prompts for Middle Grade Students*

# Bibliography

*A to Z Authentic Assessment.* Imogene Forte and Sandra Schurr. Nashville, Incentive Publications Inc., 1997.

*BASIC/Not Boring Fractions & Decimals 6-8+.* Imogene Forte and Marge Frank. Nashville, Incentive Publications Inc., 1997

*BASIC/Not Boring Geometry & Measurement Grades 6-8+.* Imogene Forte and Marge Frank. Nashville, Incentive Publications Inc., 1997

*BASIC/Not Boring Graphing, Statistics, & Probability 6-8+.* Imogene Forte and Marge Frank. Nashville, Incentive Publications Inc., 2000

*BASIC/Not Boring Middle Grades Math Book of Tests.* Imogene Forte and Marge Frank. Nashville, Incentive Publications Inc., 2000

*BASIC/Not Boring Pre-Algebra 6-8+.* Imogene Forte and Marge Frank. Nashville, Incentive Publications Inc., 2000

*BASIC/Not Boring Problem Solving Grades 6-8+.* Imogene Forte and Marge Frank. Nashville, Incentive Publications Inc., 1997

*BASIC/Not Boring Whole Numbers and Integers 6-8+.* Imogene Forte and Marge Frank. Nashville, Incentive Publications Inc., 1997

*The Definitive Middle School Guide.* Imogene Forte and Sandra Schurr. Nashville, Incentive Publications Inc., 1993

*Graphic Organizers and Planning Outlines.* Imogene Forte and Sandra Schurr. Nashville, Incentive Publications Inc., 1996

*How to Write a Great Research Paper.* Leland Graham and Darriel Ledbetter. Nashville, Incentive Publications Inc., 1994

*Integrating Instruction in Math.* Imogene Forte and Sandra Schurr. Nashville, Incentive Publications Inc., 1996

*Interdisciplinary Units and Projects for Thematic Instruction.* Nashville, Incentive Publications Inc., 1994

*Making Portfolios, Products, and Performances Meaningful and Manageable for Students and Teachers.* Imogene Forte and Sandra Schurr. Nashville, Incentive Publications Inc., 1995

*Math in the Real World of Architecture.* Shirley Cook. Nashville, Incentive Publications Inc., 1996

*Math in the Real World of Business & Living.* Shirley Cook. Nashville, Incentive Publications Inc., 1996

*Math in the Real World of Design & Art.* Shirley Cook. Nashville, Incentive Publications Inc., 1996

*Middle School Mathematician (The).* Terri Breeden and Kathryn Dillard. Nashville, Incentive Publications Inc., 1996

*Masterminds Riddle Math: Decimals, Percentages, Metric System, and Consumer Math.* Opie, Jackson, & McAvinn. Nashville, Incentive Publications Inc., 1995

*Masterminds Riddle Math: Fractions, Ratio, Probability, and Standard Measurement.* Opie, Jackson, & McAvinn. Nashville, Incentive Publications Inc., 1995

*Masterminds Riddle Math: Addition, Subtraction, Place Value, and Other Numeration Systems.* Opie, Jackson, & McAvinn. Nashville, Incentive Publications Inc., 1995

*Masterminds Riddle Math: Multiplication and Division.* Opie, Jackson, & McAvinn. Nashville, Incentive Publications Inc., 1995

*Masterminds Riddle Math: Geometry and Graphing.* Opie, Jackson, McAvinn, & Ygnve. Nashville, Incentive Publications Inc., 1995

*Masterminds Riddle Math: Pre-Algebra.* Opie & McAvinn. Nashville, Incentive Publications Inc., 1996

*Masterminds Riddle Math: Skills Boosters for the Reluctant Math Student.* Opie & McAvinn. Nashville, Incentive Publications Inc., 2000

*Reports Students Love to Write and Teachers Love to Read.* Imogene Forte and Sandra Schurr. Nashville, Incentive Publications Inc., 1999

*Tools, Treasures, and Measures.* Imogene Forte and Sandra Schurr. Nashville, Incentive Publications Inc., 1994

*Use that Computer!* Lucinda Johnston, Howard Johnston, and James Forde. Nashville, Incentive Publications Inc., 2001

*Wow, What a Team!* Randy Thompson and Dorothy VanderJagt. Nashville, Incentive Publications Inc., 2001

# Index

*Standards-Based MATH Graphic Organizers, Rubrics, and Writing Prompts for Middle Grade Students*